The Standard

# MODERN DOLL

## IDENTIFICATION & VALUE GUIDE

### 1935 - 1976

Copyright: Bill Schroeder, 1976
ISBN: 0-89145-013-0

COLLECTOR BOOKS
P. O. Box 3009
Paducah, Kentucky 42001

## DEDICATION

The editors of the Schroeder Publishing Company dedicate this volume to all collectors and dealers who not only want to know WHAT the doll is but also want to know it's VALUE.

## ACKNOWLEDGEMENTS

The editors wish to thank the following for the use of their doll pictures: Margaret Biggers, Alice Capps, Bessie Carson, Barbara Coker, Edith DeAngelo, Marie Ernst, Thelma Flack, Maxine & Robbie Heitt, Verena Holshey, Mr. J. C. Houston, Virginia Jones, Jay Minter, Marge Meisinger, Mary Partridge, Shirley Peustzer & Kathy Walters.

# HOW TO PRICE DOLLS

A PRICE GUIDE is best used as a comparison check list. The use of the word "GUIDE" is for a reason and this book is meant to be that . . . . a guide to be used as a basis of comparison for buying or selling dolls. It is not meant to be used as "set price" figures. All the prices are for above average dolls but not mint ones. MINT ones in their ORIGINAL boxes & in ULTRA PERFECT condition will bring more money.

When you are buying dolls this Price Guide should be used to compare current values for a certain doll. Let us say you are looking at a Madame Alexander's early cloth doll Oliver Twist and you see it is listed as having a value of $95.00 but the dealer is asking $100.00. If you want the doll bad enough you will go ahead and pay for it. If you don't then you will walk away.

When you are selling this Price Guide should be used to compare current prices for certain dolls. Let us say you are bidding on a doll at auction and use the same Madame Alexander doll, Oliver Twist, for example. By checking this Price Guide you know the current value is $95.00, so you can stop bidding at around $60.00 (40% is usual dealer mark up).

Please remember that a Price Guide is just that: a GUIDE.

# CONTENTS

# ADVERTISING DOLLS

15" AUNT JEMIMA. Lithograph oil cloth. Name on apron. $37.00

14" AUNT JEMIMA. Lithograph on muslin. Yellow dress with black dots. Aunt Jemima, on back. $32.00

11" GERBER BABY. All rubber. MARKS: GERBER BABY/GERBER PRODUCTS CO., on head. MFG. BY THE SUN RUBBER CO./BARBERTON, O., USA/PAT. 2118682/PAT. 2160739. $10.00

12" BUDDY LEE. All composition. Painted eyes, Jointed shoulders only. $85.00

13" BUDDY LEE. All hard plastic. Painted features. Jointed shoulders only. MARKS: BUDDY LEE, on back. $65.00

17" QUACKER CRACKELS BOY. Lithograph pale lavender suit. Green vest. Box of Quaker Crackels in hip pocket. 1928. $46.00

9" FRESH UP FREDDIE. All molded vinyl squeeze toy type. MARKS: 1959, on foot. THE/SEVEN UP/CO., on other foot & front. $24.00

15" SANTA CLAUS FOR COCA COLA. Vinyl face & hands. Boots also vinyl. Plush body. Holds Coca Cola bottle in one hand. 1956. $18.00

23" PURINA SCARECROW. Litho. cloth with vinyl head. 1965. MARKS: R.P.CO. $8.00

20" MR. PEANUT. All litho. cloth. Trademark for Planters Peanut Co. 1960's .$5.00

25" POLLY POND BEAUTY DOLL. One piece vinyl. High heels. Vinyl head. Rooted hair. Sleep eyes. 1956. MARKS: 4505 high on head. 1325-1/MADE IN USA on neck flange. Made by Citro Mfg. Co. $18.00

15" VERMONT MAID (Syrup). Full jointed vinyl. Rooted hair in twin braids. Blue sleep eyes. High heel feet. MARKS: U22 (also 18). Made by Uneeda. $14.00

14" TEDDY SNOW CROP. All terry cloth with felt features. Blue Ribbon reads: "Hi, I'm Teddy Snow Crop". $5.00

7½" SPEEDY ALKA SELTZER. One piece molded-painted vinyl. Holds a large Alka Seltzer tablet. MARKS: SPEEDY on cap. MILES LAB, on foot. ALKA SELTZER. $3.00

7½" "LI'L MISS JUSTRITE" Plastic & Vinyl. Yellow hair. Painted green eyes. MARKS: 1965 R. Dakin & Co./Prod. of Hong Kong, on head. $6.00

17" "C & H SUGAR TWINS" $4.00 each

13" "BEN" of the Franklin Life Insurance Co. $5.00

9" "PAM" as "Fab Girl" Dress identifies. Pink with white eyelet trim. $9.00

20" CHARLIE CHOCKS. Litho. cloth. MARKS: CHOCKS VITA-AMINS with bottles around waist. $8.00

20" CHICKEN OF SEA MERMAID. Vinyl head, arms & upper body. Cloth fish tail and lower body. Blonde rooted hair. Sleep blue eyes. $35.00

16" CHORE GIRL. Litho. cloth. Promotion for Chore Girl Pot Scrubbers. MARKED on front. $6.00

18" BANDY. Wood body & limbs, jointed elbows & knees. Compo. head. MARKS: GENERAL ELECTRIC/RADIO, on hat. ART QUALITY/MANU. BY CAMBO PROD. INC. etc. on foot. $45.00

8½" HEINZ BABY. Premium for Heinz Baby Food. One piece vinyl with molded on diaper, shoes & socks. Molded hair with peak above forehead "Watermelon" smile. $22.00

26" KORN KRISP. Lith. cloth. with "MY NAME IS MISS KORN KRISP" at lower waist. $32.00

10" MARKY MAYPO. Painted & molded vinyl. MARKS: MARKY MAYPO, on front of hat. $6.00

18" PETER PAN. Litho. cloth of orange, red & blue. Peter Pan Ice Cream Stores. MARKS: CHASE BAG CO. REISVILLE, N. C. $4.00

7" PHILLIPS '66 MAN. Painted & molded compo. with one piece body. Spring nodding head. Phillips '66 emblem on front. Japan in oval on base. $26.00

8" MR. CLEAN. Molded & painted vinyl. Jointed waist only. Arms folded across chest. Made in 1961 by Ideal for Proctor & Gamble. $7.00

15" RAISIN DOLL. Litho. cloth. 1973 premium for Purina's Raisin Bran Chex cereal. $5.00

12" SONY BOY. All vinyl. Molded, painted clothes & features. Jointed neck. MARKS: SONY on shirt. SONY CORP/JAPAN, on foot. $6.00

6½" SUNSHINE ELEPHANT. Litho. cloth. MARKS: TODAY/SUN-SHINE/ANIMAL/CRACKER/AT/YOUR GROCER, on blanket. $4.00

11½" TEXACO CHEERLEADER. Long blonde hair. Painted to side blue eyes. Used for Texaco Oil promotion. 1973. MARKS: T30/HONG KONG, on head. 2/MADE IN/ HONG KONG, on back. $5.00

7

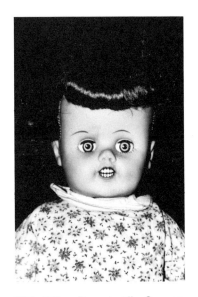

15" "Miss Pepsodent". One pc. vinyl body. Sleep eyes. Open mouth with ball. Laying down teeth are yellow, upright they are white. 1953 by Lever Bros. MARKS: A-E, on head. $45.00

17" "DERBY GAS CO."

15" "HILLBILLIE GOAT" Kellog co. $4.00

15" "VERMONT MAID" Sleep blue eyes. Red rooted hair. Made for Vermont Maid Syrup Co. MARKS: U, on head. 1964. $15.00

16" OLIVER TWIST. Stuffed cloth. Painted features. Aqua pants, orange jacket, royal blue cap. 1927. MARKS: OLIVER TWIST /MADAME ALEXANDER, etc. on tag. $95.00

14" LITTLE SHAVER. Stuffed cloth. Various colors floss wigs. Molded & painted features. $60.00

19" TIPPY TOE. Stuffed cloth. Various color mohair wigs. Molded & painted features. Tippy Toe/MADAME ALEXANDER, etc. $85.00

16" LITTLE DORRITT. Various color wigs. Molded-painted features. Stuffed cloth. Green dress with orange/white flowers. White collar. 1929. Tag: Little Dorritt, etc. $95.00

16" ALICE IN WONDERLAND. All cloth. Felt face mask. Painted features. Yellow yarn hair. Tag: Original/Alice in Wonderland /Trademark 304,488/Madame Alexander. $75.00

22" ALICE IN WONDERLAND. All cloth with face painted. Large round eyes to side. "oh" mouth. 1931. Tag: Original/Alice In Wonderland/Trademark Reg. U. S. Pat. Off. etc. $95.00

16" LITTLE WOMEN. Stuffed cloth. Buckram face mask. 1924 -1929. Tag: Little Women/Beth (or others)/Copyright Pending /Madame Alexander, etc. $50.00 each.

7" ALICE IN WONDERLAND. All compo. Painted blue eyes to side. One piece body & head. Painted on shoes & socks. Blonde mohair. MARKS: ALEXANDER, on head. Tagged dress. 1932. $38.00

7" POLLERA. All Compo. Painted blue eyes to side. Black mohair. One piece body & head. 1933. MARKS: MME ALEXANDER, on back. Tagged dress. $38.00

7" ROUND THE WORLD SERIES. All compo. One piece head & body. Painted eyes to side. Various countries, marks; MME/ ALEXANDER, on backs. 1936. $35.00 each.

19" BETTY. All compo. Brown sleep eyes. Human hair wig. Long, straight legs. Rosebud mouth. 1935. Tagged dress. $75.00

13" BETTY. All compo. Molded hair under blonde mohair. Blue sleep eyes. Painted upper lashes. Rosebud mouth. Tagged dress. $45.00

16" BABY JANE. All compo. Open mouth/5 teeth. Brown sleep eyes. Brown/red wig. MARKS: BABY JANE/REG./MME ALEXANDER, on head. $125.00

11" "WENDY ANN" All composition. Blue tin sleep eyes. Both arms are straight. MARKS: WENDY ANN/BY MADAME Alexander, on tag. 1937. $40.00

14" "WENDY ANN" All composition. MARKS: WENDY ANN on back and tag. 1937. $45.00

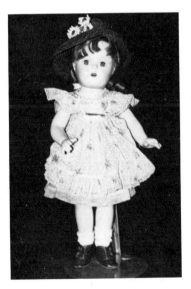

11" "MEXICO" All Composition. Painted blue eyes. Original. 1938. $40.00

15" "FLORA MCFLIMSEY" All composition and all original. 1939. $55.00

13" WENDY ANN. All compo. Swivel waist. Sleep eyes. Molded hair. MARKS: WENDY ANN/MME ALEXANDER/NEW YORK. $45.00

13" WENDY ANN. All compo. Swivel waist. Molded hair. Painted eyes. MARKS: WENDY ANN/MME ALEXANDER/NEW YORK. $35.00

14" JEANNIE WALKER. All compo. with wood crotch joined to body with screws. Brown sleep eyes. Rosebud mouth. MARKS: ALEXANDER/PAT. NO. 2171281, on back. $85.00 18":$100.00. Available from 1939 through 1943.

20" PINKY. (Baby) Cloth & compo. Molded hair. Sleep eyes. MARKS: MME ALEXANDER, on head. Tagged clothes. $65.00

14" W.A.V.E. or W.A.A.C. All compo. Wigged but came with painted or sleep eyes. MARKS: MME ALEXANDER, on head. Tagged clothes. $75.00

17" WEDDING PARTY BRIDE. All compo. Sleep blue eyes. MARKS: MME ALEXANDER, on head. Tag: BRIDE/MADAME ALEXANDER, etc. $65.00. 18" $75.00. 22" $95.00

15" BRIDESMAID. All compo. Sleep blue eyes. MARKS: MME ALEXANDER, on head. TAG: BRIDESMAID/MADAME ALEXANDER, etc. $65.00. 18" $75.00. 22" $95.00

16" FLOWERGIRL. All compo. Sleep blue eyes. Open mouth/teeth. MARKS: PRINCESS ELIZABETH/MADAME ALEXANDER CO., on head. 1945. $65.00. 20" $85.00. 24" $115.00

14" CARMEN MIRANDA. All compo. Black mohair wig. Sleep eyes. 2 piece costume. MARKS: MME ALEXANDER, on head. $65.00 21" $95.00

14" MARGARET O'BRIEN. All Compo. Pigtail wig. Brown sleep eyes. MARKS: ALEXANDER, on head. Tagged clothes. 1946. $125.00. 18" $165.00. 21" $185.00

14" SONJA HENIE. All compo. Sleep brown eyes. Open mouth. Dimples. MARKS: MADAME ALEXANDER/SONJA HENIE, on head. Tagged clothes. 1939-1944. $75.00. 18" $85.00. 21" $95.00

13" CLOSED MOUTH JANE WITHERS. All compo. Deep red brown mohair wig. Hazel sleep eyes. MARKS: JANE WITHERS /ALEXANDER DOLL CO., on head. 1937. $145.00

17" JANE WITHERS. All compo. Green sleep eyes. Open mouth. MARKS: 17, on back. Tagged clothes. 1937. $125.00. 21" $165.00

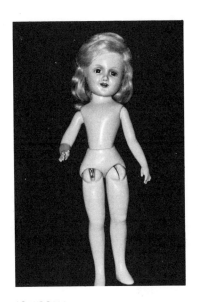

18" "SCARLET" All composition and all original. 1940. $85.00

13""SONJA HENIE"All composition. Jointed waist. Dimples. Black eyeshadow. MARKS: ALEXANDER/NEW YORK, on back. L, back of left leg & R, back of right leg. 1940. $65.00

14" All composition and all original "Scarlet". 1941. $70.00

15" "KATE GREENAWAY" All composition. Sleep blue eyes. MARKS: PRINCESS ELIZABETH /MADAME ALEXANDER, on head. All original. 1941. $75.00

ALEXANDER

15" PRINCESS ELIZABETH. All compo. Sleep eyes. Open mouth. MARKS: PRINCESS ELIZABETH/ALEXANDER DOLL CO. Tagged dress: $60.00. 12" $50.00. 18" $65.00. 20" $75.00. 24" $85.00

7½" DIONNE QUINT BABY. All compo. Bent baby legs. MARKS: ALEXANDER, on head & back. Molded hair & painted eyes. $200.00 set.

7½" DIONNE QUINT BABY. Wigged with painted eyes. $225.00 set.

8" DIONNE QUINT TODDLERS. All compo. Toddler legs. Molded hair. Painted eyes. Marked. $200.00 set.

8" DIONNE QUINT TODDLERS. Wigged with painted eyes. $225.00 set.

11" DIONNE QUINT BABY. All compo. Molded hair. Sleep eyes. Bent baby legs. Marked. $75.00 each. Some will measure 10".

11" DIONNE QUINT TODDLER. All compo. Toddler legs. Wigged with sleep eyes. Marked. $75.00 each.

14" DIONNE QUINT TODDLER. All compo. Wigs. Sleep eyes. Marked. $85.00 each.

16" DIONNE QUINT TODDLER. All compo. Wigs. Sleep eyes. Marked. $85.00 each.

19" DIONNE QUINT TODDLER. All compo. Wigs. Sleep eyes. Marked. $95.00 each.

20" DIONNE QUINT TODDLER. All compo. Wigs. Sleep eyes. Marked. $95.00 each.

23" DIONNE QUINT TODDLER. All compo. Wigs. Sleep eyes. Marked. $100.00 each.

24" DIONNE QUINT. All stuffed pink stockenette body & limbs. Molded felt face mask. Painted features. $125.00 each.

11" FAIRY PRINCESS. All compo. Shoulder length blonde wig. Sleep eyes. Rosebud mouth. MARKS: MME ALEXANDER, on head. Tagged clothes. $40.00. 15" $45.00. 18" $50.00. 22" $60.00

11" SOUTHERN GIRL. All compo. Sleep eyes. Rosebud mouth. Southern clothes with pantaloons. MARKS: MME ALEX-ANDER. Tagged clothes. $55.00. 15" $60.00. 18" $65.00. 22" $65.00

21" "JANE WITHERS" All composition. Original. 1936. $165.00

10" "LITTLE SHAVER" Came as blonde or brunette. Pink or yellow skirt. 1937. $60.00

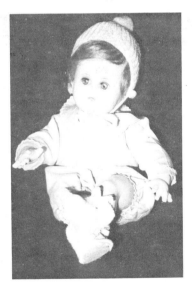

16" "DIONNE QUINT" Prices listed on opposite page. 1937.

11" "BUTCH" Cloth & Composition. Sleep blue eyes. MARKS: MME. ALEXANDER, on head. TAG: BUTCH/ MADAME ALEXANDER. 1938. $35.00

10" SO-LITE. All pink cloth with molded hardened cloth face with painted features. Kinky yellow yarn hair. Tagged. $35.00. 12" $35.00. 18" $45.00. 20" $45.00. 24" $50.00

24" SPECIAL GIRL. Cloth body. Compo. head & limbs. Long blonde braids. Closed mouth. Long straight legs. Tagged dress. $85.00

14½" MARY MARTIN. All hard plastic. Lambs wool wig. Sleep eyes. Sailor suit with name on front. MARKS: none. Tag: MARY MARTIN/OF SOUTH PACIFIC/MADAME ALEXANDER etc. 1948. $85.00

18" PRINCE PHILLIP. All hard plastic. Lambs wool wig. Tuxedo. Sleep eyes. MARKS: none. TAG: MADAME ALEXANDER, etc. $95.00

15" BABS THE ICE SKATER. Hard plastic with mohair wig. Sleep eyes. 1948. MARKS: ALEXANDER, on head. Tagged clothes. $45.00. 18" $65.00

17" MARGARET ROSE. All hard plastic. Human hair wig. Sleep eyes. 1949. MARKS: ALEXANDER, on head. Tagged clothes. $50.00

15" SNOW WHITE. All hard plastic. Black wig. Sleep eyes. Gown of pink and gold with gold jacket tied in front. $40.00. 18" $50.00. 23" $70.00

15" LITTLE WOMEN. All hard plastic. Sleep eyes. MARKS: ALEXANDER, on backs. Tagged clothes. $275.00 set.

15" LITTLE MEN. All hard plastic. Sleep eyes. MARKS: ALEXANDER, on backs. Tagged clothes. $60.00 each.

18" WINNIE WALKER. All hard plastic. Synthetic wig. Blue sleep eyes. Standard walking mechanism. 1953. Looks like a Cissy. Tagged clothes. $40.00

14" CYNTHIA. (colored). All brown hard plastic. Brown sleep eyes. 1952. MARKS: ALEX., on head. Tagged clothes. $85.00

15" LOVEY-DOVEY. (baby). Molded brown hair. Sleep blue eyes. Stuffed latex body & limbs. Hard plastic head. Tagged clothes. $35.00

29" BARBARA JANE. Stuffed early vinyl limbs & head. Cloth body. Rooted hair. Sleep eyes. Long arms & legs. MARKS: ALEXANDER, on head. Tagged clothes. $95.00

16" BUD. Cloth body, early vinyl limbs & head. Rooted boy cut hair. Blue sleep eyes. Closed mouth. MARKS: ALEXANDER, on head. Tagged clothes. 1952. $45.00

12½" "SNOW WHITE" All composition. Original. MARKS: MME. ALEXANDER, on head. 1939. $60.00

18" "SONJA HENIE" Original. All composition. 1941. $75.00

Wendy (8") with push buttons to nod head. This is one of the "QUIZ KIDS". All hard plastic. 1954. $50.00

15" "CISSY" Hard plastic walker. Vinyl arms over plastic. Jointed elbows. MARKS: ALEXANDER, on head. 1955. $25.00

15" BALLERINA ELISE. Hard plastic with vinyl head. Rooted hair. Blue sleep eyes. Jointed knees & ankles. MARKS: ALEX., on head. Tagged clothes. $35.00. 18" $45.00

15" ROSAMUND. All hard plastic. Walker, head turns. Glued on wig. Sleep eyes. MARKS: ALEX., on head. Tagged clothes. Has Kathy & Annabelle face. $42.00. 18" $48.00

15" PETER PAN. All hard plastic. Glued on short hair. Sleep eyes. Same face as Kathy and Annabelle. One size only. $50.00

15" WENDY. Of Peter Pan. All hard plastic. Glued on wig. Sleep eyes. Dressed in blue satin. Elise face. MARKS: ALEX., on head, Tagged clothes. One size. $45.00

15" MISS FLORA MCFLIMSEY. Hard plastic body & limbs. Vinyl head. Rooted hair. Sleep eyes. MARKS: ALEXANDER, on head. Tagged clothes. Cissy face. One size only. $50.00

18" QUEEN ELIZABETH. All hard plastic. Walker. Sleep eyes. Elise face. White brocade gown, jewelery. Long velvet robe. Tiara. MARKS: ALEX., on head. Tagged clothes. $60.00

18" PRINCESS MARGARET ROSE. All hard plastic. Walker. Sleep eyes. Elise face. Pink Taffeta gown. Tiara. Long white gloves. MARKS: ALEX., on head. Tagged clothes. $50.00

18" VICTORIA. All hard plastic. Walker. Blue taffeta with side panniers & bustle, with narrow white braid. Kathy face. MARKS: ALEX., Tagged clothes. $45.00

7½" VICTORIA. All hard plastic. Walker. Dressed same as doll above. (Me & My Shadow Series.) MARKS: ALEX., on back. Tagged clothes. $35.00

18" MARY LOUISE. All hard plastic. Walker. Taffeta gown of Burnt Sugar. Jacket & hat of olive green. Cissy face. MARKS: ALEX. Tagged clothes. $45.00

7½" MARY LOUISE. All hard plastic. Walker. Dressed same as doll above. (Me & My Shadow Series) MARKS: ALEX., on back. Tagged dress. $35.00

18" ELAINE. All hard plastic. Walker. Garden dress of pale blue organdy. Rows of lace. Under dress of pink taffeta. White taffeta hoop skirt. Neck outlined with pearls. Blue satin sash. Picture straw hat. Tagged dress. Cissy face. $45.00

7½" ELAINE. All hard plastic. Walker. Dressed same as doll above. (Me & My Shadow Series). MARKS: ALEX., on back. Tagged dress. $35.00

10" Latex one piece body, arms and legs. Original. MARKS: ALEX-ANDER, on head. MADAME ALEXANDER, on tag. 1952. $18.00

10" Latex one piece body, arms and legs. Original. MARKS: ALEX-ANDER, on head. TAG: MADAM ALEXANDER. 1952. $16.00

22" "ROSEBUD" 1953. Cloth body with cryer. Vinyl head, arms and legs. Molded hair. Sleep blue eyes. MARKS: ALEXANDER, on head. 1953. $22.00

14½" "STORY PRINCESS" All hard plastic with green sleep eyes. 1956. $60.00

15" STORY PRINCESS. All hard plastic. Sleep eyes. Jointed knees. Cissy face. Magenta dress & net overskirt. MARKS: ALEX., on head. $60.00

31" MARY ELLEN. Plastic body & limbs. Vinyl head. Rooted hair. Sleep eyes. MARKS: ALEXANDER, on head. Tagged clothes. $85.00

9" CISSETE. All hard plastic. Sleep eyes. Jointed knees. Some are walkers & head turns. MARKS: MME ALEXANDER, on back. Tagged clothes. $30.00

9" SLEEPING BEAUTY. All hard plastic. Blue sleep eyes. Flat feet. Turquoise dress with gold trim. MARKS: MME ALEXANDER, on back. Tagged dress. $30.00

28" ALICE IN WONDERLAND. Cloth body. Early stuffed vinyl head & limbs. Long thin arms & legs. 1955. MARKS: ALEXANDER, on head. Tagged dress. $95.00

20" CISSY PORTRAIT. 1955. Hard plastic with vinyl oversleeved arms. Jointed knees & elbows. Came in 7 outfits: 1. Gown in white organdy trimmed with lace & roses. Straw picture hat. 2. Gown of champagne satin. Muff. 3. As Queen in white brocade. Jewelery & tiara. 4. Gown of blue satin. Coronet of flowers & jewels. Ostrich fan. 5. Gown of gold taffeta & matching short evening coat trimmed in gold braid. Gold hoop earrings. 6. Bridal outfit in white brocade. Veil of nylon tulle on coronet. Carries white tulle muff decorated with blossoms. 7. Long torso gown of mauve taffeta with huge bow of mauve, green & gold striped taffeta. $65.00 each.

20" CISSY FASHION PARADE. Hard plastic with vinyl oversleeved arms. Jointed knees and elbows. 1956 came in 8 outfits: I. Garden party gown of organdy trimmed with rosebuds & big organdy sash. Wide brim straw hat. 2. Ankle length gown of pink nylon tulle. Corsage at waist. Wide pink sash. Flowers in hair. 3. Bridesmaid gown of nylon tulle with silver threaded net in blue. Hat of fluffy tulle with rosebuds. 4. Bride in white tulle with finely pleated skirt. Lace bodice. Satin sash pulled through loops of pearls. Chapel length veil. 5. Queen Elizabeth. Gown of white brocade is over a hoop petticoat of taffeta. Tiara & jewels. 6. Long torso gown of pink taffeta. Diagonal side drapery held in place by jeweled ornaments. Flowers in hair. 7. Ball gown of satin with side drapery over billowy petticoat of taffeta. "Fur" shoulder cape is satin lined. 8. Black velvet gown with "waist" at hips. Flares out below hips. Lined with pink satin. V neck with cluster of roses. $60.00 each.

12" "MARME" All hard plastic. 1957. $25.00

12" "LISSY" Shown in an original dress. TAG: LISSY BY MADAME ALEXANDER. 1956. $35.00

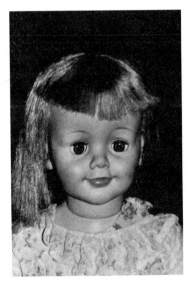

12" "LISSY" shown in pink formal and straw hat. 1957. $35.00

30" "BETTY" Plastic & vinyl. Flirty sleep eyes. Head sockets into neck. Posable head. MARKS: ALEXANDER/1959. $80.00

14" SLUMBERMATE. Cloth body & limbs. Vinyl head. Eyes closed. Open "yawn" mouth. MARKS: ALEX., on head. Tagged clothes. $30.00

18½"BUNNY BABY. Cloth body. Early vinyl head & limbs. Sleep blue eyes. Open mouth/two upper teeth. MARKS: ALEXANDER, on head. Tagged clothes. $50.00

18" MCGUFFEY ANA. Cissy doll with blonde braids. Velveteen jumper, nylon blouse, hoop petticoat. Matching bonnet. High button shoes. $40.00. 25" $75.00 1956.

20" CISSY MODELS FORMAL GOWNS. 1957. 8 outfits: l. Formal gown of black velvet cut on princess lines. Cape of "fur". Corsage of roses. Long black gloves. 2. Gold brocade court gown. Tiara. Long white gloves. 3. Taffeta gown with elbow length puff sleeves. Large flower trimmed picture hat. 4. Bride in white nylon tulle with double train of white satin. Chapel length veil with coronet of flowers. Bodice of satin applique. Long gloves. 5. Dressed as Lady Hamilton. Floor length bouffant skirt, over half slip of nylon. Draped bodice & skirt are trimmed with tiny pink roses. Large picture hat. 6. Floor length dress of dotted nylon net over pink taffeta. Large hat of horsehair braid trimmed with flowers. Wide satin sash hangs to floor in back. 7. Gown of purple velvet with long tight fitting torso. Flare of layers of lilac nylon tulle. Bunch of pink roses at skirt line. 8. Lace print on heavy faille with wide circular skirt (lined). Velvet sash caught at the waistline with a corsage of roses. Cape stole of "fur" is satin lined. $55.00 each.

20" CISSY IN CLASSIC GOWNS. 1958. 6 outfits. 1. Floor length full skirt, fitted bodice. Sleeveless net overskirt. Large picture hat trimmed with roses. 2. Bride with lace gown embroidered with bridal wreath pattern. Full length veil of tulle attached to coronet of flowers. 3. Calf length cocktail dress of satin. Flowers in hair. Bouffant stole of tulle & shortie gloves. 4. Hollyberry red floor length dress of taffeta. Wide skirt. Tulle stole with irridescent dots. 5. Queen in gold brocade. Gold tiara. 6. Ball gown with printed camellias on silk. Long cape stole of velvet lined to match. Hat with face veil. $50.00 each.

35" JOANIE. Heavy vinyl body. Vinyl head. Flirty blue eyes. Smile closed mouth. Walker. MARKS: ALEXANDER/1959, on head. Tagged clothes. $110.00

36" JANIE. Heavy vinyl body. Vinyl head. Sleep blue eyes. MARKS: ALEXANDER/1959 on head. Tagged clothes. $95.00

15" STORY PRINCESS. All hard plastic. Sleep eyes. Elise face. Two layer blue taffeta dress. Tiara & wand. MARKS: tagged dress. $50.00. 18" $55.00

21" "JACQULINE" Original riding habit. Same doll as used for the Portrait series. 1962. $150.00 in this outfit only.

12" "JANIE" Plastic & vinyl. Blue sleep eyes. Original. MARKS: ALEXANDER/1964, on head. TAG: JANIE/MADAME ALEXANDER. $38.00

12" "JANIE BALLERINA" Plastic & vinyl. 1964. $38.00

17" "POLLY" Plastic & vinyl. Original. MARKS: ALEXANDER DOLL CO/1965, on head. $30.00

30" BETTY. Body & limbs of So-Lite plastic. Vinyl head same as Joanie. Flirty eyes. Walker. MARKS: ALEXANDER/1959, on head. $80.00

16" MAGGIE MIXUP. All vinyl. Brick red hair. Green sleep eyes. Jointed elbows & knees. Freckles. MARKS: ALEXANDER, on head. MME ALEXANDER, on back. $55.00

21" SCARLETT O'HARA. (Cissy doll). Taffeta gown with braid trim worn over billowing crinoline petticoat. Lace mitts & velvet purse. $75.00. 1961

21" MELANIE. (Cissy doll). 1961. Gown of stiff slipper satin with overdress of lace. Hairdo in Godey fashion. $75.00

21" JACQUELINE. Plastic body & legs. Vinyl arms & head. Rooted brunette hair. Brown sleep eyes. Same doll as used for later portraits. MARKS: ALEXANDER 1961, on head. TAG: JAC-QUELINE/MADAME ALEXANDER, etc. $125.00. In tagged riding outfit: $150.00

14" CAROLINE. Plastic & vinyl. Green sleep eyes. Open/closed mouth. MARKS: ALEXANDER/1961, on head. TAG: CAROL-INE/MADAME ALEXANDER, etc. $65.00. In riding habit $85.00

10" JACQUELING. All rigid plastic. Sleep eyes. (This is Cissette doll). Brunette wig. MARKS: MME ALEXANDER, on back. TAG: JACQUELINE/MADAME ALEXANDER, etc. $45.00

12" LITTLE WOMEN. All are Lissy dolls. All hard plastic. Sleep eyes. Glued on wigs. MARKS: ALEX., on back. Tagged clothes. $225.00 set.

30" MIMI. Plastic & vinyl. Jointed in 12 places. Flirty sleep eyes. MARKS: ALEXANDER/1961, on head. $125.00

12" SMARTY. Boy or girl. Plastic body & limbs. Vinyl head. Sleep eyes. Open/closed mouth. MARKS: ALEXANDER/1962. Tagged clothes. $38.00

23" SWEETIE WALKER. Plastic & vinyl. Rooted blonde hair in short straight hair with full bangs. Fat toddler arms & legs. MARKS: ALEXANDER. $40.00

12" SOUTHERN BELLE. (Lissy doll). All hard plastic. Satin calf length dress with 3 rows lace at bottom. Lace edges pantolettes. Blonde hair in long curls. Hat trimmed in feathers. $45.00. 1963

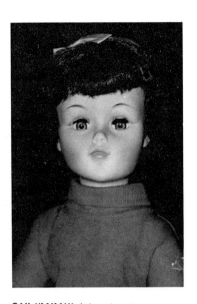

29" All stuffed vinyl. Sleep blue eyes. MARKS: ALEXANDER, on head. Used for several personalities. 1955. $95.00

31" "MIMI" Jointed waist, elbows, wrists, knees & ankles. Plastic & vinyl. MARKS: ALEXANDER/ 1961. $125.00

21" "RENOIR" in pink and black. Plastic & vinyl. MARKS: ALEXANDER 1961, on head. $125.00

12" "PAMELA" Hard plastic with vinyl head. Came with three wigs. MARKS: ALEXANDER/1962. $60.00

12" SCARLETT O'HARA. (Lissy doll). All hard plastic. Floor length green taffeta gown with matching bonnet. 1963. $45.00

12" MCGUFFEY ANA. (Lissy doll) 1963. Red velvet suit with circular lined skirt. White fur-like hat, jacket, collar & mittens. Black shoes with buttoned gaiters. $45.00

18" QUEEN ELIZABETH. 1963. (Elise doll). Jointed ankles. $50.00

18" SCARLETT. 1963. (Elise doll). Jointed ankles. $70.00

18" RENOIR PORTRAIT. 1963. (Elise doll). Jointed ankles. $50.00

1965 was the introduction of the 21" Portraits using the JACQUELINE doll. They are all marked: ALEXANDER 1961: All have tagged clothes. 1966 was the only year they used the COCO doll for Portraits.

1965: No. 2151: BRIDE, No. 2152: SCARLETT, No. 2153: GODEY, No. 2154: RENOIR, No. 2155: SOUTHERN BELLE, No. 2150: QUEEN.

1966: (COCO): No. 2060: Madame Doll, No. 2063: Godey, No. 2050: Melanie, No. 2061: Scarlett, No. 2051: Lissy, No. 2062: Renoir, Coco only $150.00 each.

1967: No. 2174: Scarlett, No. 2175: Renoir, No. 2170: Southern Belle, No. 2172: Godey, No. 2173: Melanie, No. 2171: Agatha.

1968: No. 2182: Lady Hamilton, No. 2181: Melanie, No. 2185: Queen, No. 2180: Scarlett, No. 2184: Gainsborough, No. 2183: Goya.

1969: No. 2193: Melanie, No. 2195: Godey, No. 2192: Bride, No. 2191: Jenny Lind, No. 2190: Scarlett, No. 2194: Renoir.

1970: No. 2181: Jenny Lind, No. 2184: Renoir, No. 2196: Melanie, No. 2195: Godey, No. 2197: Madame Pompadour, No. 2180: Scarlett.

1971: No. 2170: Mimi, No. 2165: Renoir, No. 2162: Melanie, No. 2161: Godey.

1972: No. 2191: Cornella, No. 2190: Renoir, No. 2192: Gainsborough.

1973: No. 2190: Renoir, No. 2191: Cornelia, No. 2192: Gainsborough.

1974: No. 2296: Cornelia, No. 2295: Melanie, No. 2297: Agatha.

Even if some of the numbers repeat themselves, each and every Portrait is dressed differently. All Portraits: $125.00 each.

14" ORPHAN ANNIE. Plastic with vinyl head. Sleep eyes. Center parted blonde hair. Freckles. Calico print dress with lace edged organdy apron. Two button black/white shoes. $45.00

18" SITTING PRETTY. All vinyl. Fat cheeks, closed, smile/mouth. Body is covered with jersey. Wired for posing. MARKS: ALEXANDER/1964. $18.00

15" STORY PRINCESS. 1955. All hard plastic. Glued on wig. Sleep eyes. Shell pink taffeta gown. Sequins at neckline. Rosebuds on skirt. Tiara. One size only. MARKS: ALEX., on back. Tagged dress. $45.00

8" "WENDY-KIN" All hard plastic. Same as the "Alexander-Kin". 1965. $20.00

21" "COCO" one of the rarest dolls by this company. Plastic and vinyl. Legs molded in "model" position. MARKS: ALEXANDER/ 1966, on head. $150.00

8" "MISS UNITED STATES" All hard plastic. This is the first issued one. 1966 to 1968. Discontinued. $50.00

12" "NANCY DREW" Plastic & vinyl. Original. 1967. $40.00

12" BITSEY & BUTCH. Cloth body. Vinyl head & limbs. Baby legs. Sleep eyes. MARKS: ALEXANDER/1964, on heads. $16.00 each.

1965: SOUND OF MUSIC DOLLS: 17" MARIA (this is a new doll), 11" Gretl., 14" Louisa, 11" Frederich, 14" Brigitta, 14" Liesl, 11" Marta. $165.00 set.

17" MARLO THOMAS. (Same doll as Maria). Plastic & vinyl. Black eyes. MARKS: ALEXANDER/1966, on head. Tagged clothes. $65.00

8" LITTLE WOMEN. (Wendy/Alexander-kin doll). All hard plastic, jointed knees. MARKS: ALEX., on backs. Tagged clothes. $135.00 set.

8" DISCONTINUED DOLLS. All hard plastic. JOINTED KNEES. African, Amish boy & girl, Argentine boy, Bolivia. Spanish boy, Cowgirl & cowboy, Ecuador, English Guard, Eskimo, Hawaiian, Greek boy, Indian boy, Hiawatha, Indian girl, Pocahantas, Korea, American girl, McGuffey Ana, Miss U.S.A. (1968), Morocco, Peruvian boy, Priscilla, Colonial girl, Scarlett O'Hara (1965), Vietnam. Quiz Kids: $50.00 each.

8" ROUND THE WORLD OR NURSERY RHYME SERIES. All hard plastic. ALL HAVE BENDING KNEES, which has been discontinued. $18.00 each.

In 1968 Alexander brought out the 11" PORTRETTE SERIES using the Cissette doll. These have been discontinued.

1968: No. 1172: Godey, No. 1171: Agatha, No. 1174: Scarlett, No. 1170: Southern Belle, No. 1175: Renoir, No. 1173: Melinda.
1969: No. 1175: Renoir, No. 1171: Jenny Lind, No. 1174: Scarlett, No. 1170: Southern Belle, No. 1172: Godey, No. 1173: Melinda.
1970: No. 1180: Renoir, No. 1182: Melanie, No. 1181: Scarlett, No. 1183: Godey, No. 1184: Jenny Lind, No. 1185: Southern Belle.
1971: No. 1181: Scarlett, No. 1185: Southern Belle
1972: No. 1185: Southern Belle, No. 1181: Scarlett, No. 1186: Queen (This year Southern Belle & Scarlett are same as 1971).
1973: No. 1184: Southern Belle, No. 1180: Scarlett, No. 1187: Queen. Same dolls as 1972 with different numbers.
1974: Discontinued: All Portrettes: $45.00 each.

12" ROZY. (Same doll used for Smarty). Plastic & vinyl. Sleep eyes. Closed mouth. MARKS: ALEXANDER 1964, on head. (Issued in 1969). Tagged clothes. $20.00

14" "RENOIR GIRL" White dress with red trim. Plastic & vinyl. 1967. $35.00

8" "JAPANESE" All hard plastic. Both original. One has the Wendy face and other has the "Maggie Mixup" face. 1968 to date. Both have bending knees. $18.00 each.

9" "TINKER BELL" Hard plastic. Jointed knees. Came with Peter Pan set. 1971. $40.00

8" "SNOW WHITE" All hard plastic. Original. 1971. $35.00

18" BABY PETITE. Cloth with compo. head & limbs. Inset green eyes. Open/closed mouth & two teeth. 1927. MARKS: PETITE /AMER. CHAR. DOLL CO. $38.00

18" HONEY CHILD. Excelsior stuffed cloth body & legs. Compo. Shoulder plate & arms. Painted eyes. Closed mouth. Looks like Bye-lo. MARKS: HONEY CHILD. $65.00

23" WONDER BABY. Composition, bent leg baby. Blue tin sleep eyes. MARKS: PETITE/AMERICA'S WONDER BABY DOLLS. $55.00

16" SALLY. Excelsior stuffed cloth body. Compo swivel shoulder head, limbs. Straight legs. Molded "Patsy type" hair & also with wigs. MARKS: PETITE/SALLY. $38.00

20" BOTTLETOT. Cloth body & legs. Compo. arms & head. Sleep eyes. Molded hair. Hands molded for bottle. MARKS: BABY B/PETITE. $45.00

24" PERFECT BEAUTY. Stuffed body. Long straight compo. legs, compo. shoulder, head, arms (right bent). Sleep eyes. Open mouth/two teeth. MARKS: PETITE/PERFECT BEAUTY. $65.00

10½" MARVEL TOT(also HAPPY TOT). All rubber. Bent baby legs. Bent arms with palms down. Face changes from smile, pout to pucker by turning head. 1936. MARKS: AMER. CHAR. DOLL, on head. $23.00

18" TOODLES. All compo. Bent baby legs. Molded hair. Sleep tin eyes. Painted lashes over & below. Nurser. 1940. MARKS: TOODLES, on head. AMER. CHAR. DOLL, on back. $30.00

19" BABY SUE. Cloth body. Early vinyl limbs. Vinyl head. Came with molded hair or wig. Sleep eyes. Open/closed smile mouth /two molded-in teeth & tongue. 1953. MARKS: AMER. CHAR. DOLL, on head. $25.00

17" BABY SUE. Cloth body. Early latex limbs. Hard plastic head. Came with molded hair or wigs. Closed mouth. 1949. MARKS: TAG: BABY SUE/AMER. CHAR. $30.00

18" CHUCKLES (Peepers Show Baby). All vinyl. Bent baby legs. Rooted hair. Sleep eyes. Open/closed mouth with molded tongue. 1957. MARKS: Some AMER. CHAR. DOLL. on head & body. Others: NBC/AMERICAN DOLL and some with just a paper tag: CHUCKLES. $40.00

13" "CAROL ANN BERRY" All composition with mohair over molded hair. Sleep brown eyes. MARKS: PETITE, on head and body. Daughter of Actor Wallace Berry. 1935. $65.00

22" "SWEET SUE" All hard plastic walker. Flat feet. MARKS: none. 1955. $45.00

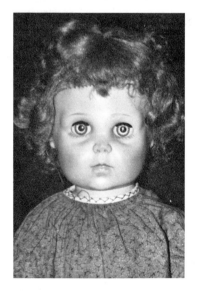

24" "DALE EVANS" Hard plastic "Sweet Sue" doll. Boots are replaced. 1955. $35.00

23" "BARBARA SUE" All vinyl with disc jointed arms. One piece body & legs. Sleep blue. MARKS: AMER. CHAR., on head. 1955. $22.00

15" SWEET SUE. All hard plastic. Walker, head turns. Inset skull cap hair. Dressed in ballgown: $28.00. 18" $30.00. 22" $35.00. 25" $40.00

10" TONI. Hard plastic. High heel feet. Vinyl head. Rooted hair. Sleep eyes. MARKS: AMER. CHAR. DOLL CORP/1958 in circle. $16.00

20" SWEET SUE. All rigid vinyl. Rooted hair. Sleep eyes. Jointed waist. High heel feet. 1954. MARKS: AMERICAN CHARACTER, in circle. Many not marked. $28.00

20" SWEET SUE. 1955. Same as above only has jointed ankles (Ballerina) came in 18" $26.00. 22" $30.00. 25" $35.00

14" TOODLES BABY. All vinyl. Rooted hair. Sleep eyes. Closed mouth. MARKS: AMERICAN CHARACTER DOLL 1958, on head. $20.00. 16" $22.00

18" TOODLE LOO. Soft foam plastic. Painted brown eyes. Closed mouth. Arms & legs flanged into body. Short stubby legs & arms. MARKS: AMERICAN DOLL & TOY CO. 1961. $30.00

10" POPI. Rigid plastic with molded hair. Has 3 vinyl wigs. Painted eyes. Pops apart at bustline & waist. Clothes are cut, drape & shape (no sewing). Had 17 outfits. 1961-62. $18.00

20" BUTTERBALL. All vinyl. Rooted hair. Sleep eyes. Closed mouth with upper lip over lower one. Short stubby fingers. MARKS: 1961/ AMERICAN DOLL & TOY CORP., in circle, on head. $30.00

23" BABY BABBLES. Same head as Butterball. Cloth body over foam. Battery operated. Electronic press to talk. Action operates with hug or squeeze. Vinyl head & limbs. MARKS: AMER. DOLL CO., on head. $45.00

30" LITTLE MISS ECHO. Plastic with vinyl head. Rooted hair. Open/closed mouth. Painted upper teeth. Battery operated tape recorder. Repeats things said to her. 1961. MARKS: none. $50.00

20" PITTIE PAT. All vinyl. Same head as Butterball & Baby Babbles. Battery operated. When hugged, her heart beats & pulses 60 or 70 times per minute. MARKS: AMERICAN DOLL & TOY CORP./1961, in circle on head. $45.00

23" SWEET SUE WALKER. Hard plastic. Walker lens. Jointed knees. Vinyl arms. Jointed elbows. Sleep eyes. Inset skull cap wig. 1954. MARKS: AMER. CHAR. DOLLS. $40.00

20" "SWEET SUE" Plastic & vinyl.
Sleep blue eyes. MARKS: none.
1960. $18.00

23" "CHUCKLES" All vinyl.
Brown painted eyes. MARKS:
1961/AMERICAN DOLL & TOY
CORP. $40.00

20" "TONI" All vinyl with flirty
eyes. MARKS: AMERICAN CHAR-
ACTER, in circle above waist.
1961. $22.00

14" "PRE-TEEN TRESSY" Plastic
& vinyl. Blue sleep eyes. Grow
hair mechanism through middle of
body. MARKS: AM. CHAR. 1963,
on head. $16.00

21″ WHIMSIE. MARKS: WHIMSIE/AMER. DOLL & TOY CO. Tillie, Bashful Bride, Graduate, Angel, Strongman, Zack, Football, Monk. All $35.00 each.

21″ WHIMSIE. MARKS: same. Tina the Cleaner, Girl Devil, Raggie, Wheeler the Dealer & Miss Take. All $45.00 each.

6″ WHIMETTES. Painted eyes/molded lids. All vinyl. Closed smile. MARKS: MADE IN HONG KONG, on head. Also marked: AMER. CHAR. '63, on head. Granny, Minnie Mod. Jump N Gogo, Pixie & Swinger. $4.00 each.

14″ PRE-TEEN TRESSY. Plastic & vinyl. Button in stomach to operate grow hair. Sleep blue eyes. MARKS: AM. CHAR. '63, on head. $12.00

12″ TRESSY. Plastic & vinyl. Painted eyes. High heel feet. Grow hair. MARKS: AMERICAN DOLL & TOY CORP/1963, in circle. $8.00

12″ POSIN TRESSY. Same as above only wired arms & legs for posing. 1966. $10.00

9½″ CRICKET. Plastic & vinyl. Grow hair feature. Painted blue eyes. Wired legs for bending. MARKS: AMERICAN CHARACTER/ 1964. $10.00

12″ MARY MAKE UP. Plastic & vinyl. Same doll as Posin Tressy with rooted white hair. Came with make up. 1966. $10.00

17″ MARGARET ROSE. Plastic & vinyl. Blonde rooted hair. Straight legs. Blue sleep eyes. MARKS: AMER. CHAR./1966. $6.00

13″ FRECKLES. Plastic & vinyl. Painted brown eyes. Freckles. Walker & face changes by moving left arm. MARKS: AMER. CHAR. INC./1966. $7.00

8″ HOSS CARTRIGHT. All rigid vinyl with molded on clothes. MARKS: LARGE C, AMERICAN CHARACTER, on back. 1966. $40.00

8″ LITTLE JOE CARTRIGHT. Same as above. Brown molded hair. $35.00

8″ OUTLAW. Same as above. Black mustache. $25.00

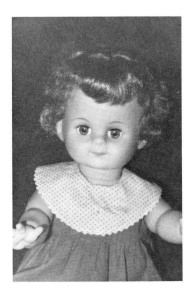

19" "SALLY SAYS" Battery operated talker. Plastic & vinyl. MARKS:
AMERICAN DOLL & TOY CORP.
/1964. $12.00

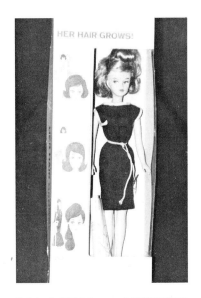

Original 1964 issue of "TRESSY"
Style no.1200. $8.00

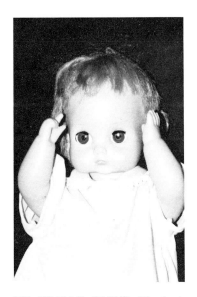

18" "SUGAR BABY" All vinyl.
Sleep brown eyes. Same body
as used for "New Tiny Tears".
MARKS: AMERICAN CHAR.
CO./1966. $14.00

8" "BEN CARTWRIGHT" All rigid
vinyl. Molded on clothes except
hat. MARKS: C/AMERICAN
CHARACTER/1966. $35.00

13" BOTTLETOT. All composition with celluloid jointed right hand. Molded-painted hair. Blue tin sleep eyes. Some unmarked: Others: ARRANBEE/PAT. Aug. 10, 26. $45.00

14" KEWTY. All composition. Molded-painted red-brown hair. Blue tin sleep eyes. Open mouth/two teeth. 1929. MARKS: KEWTY, on back. $32.00

17" NANCY. All composition. Mohair wig. Brown sleep eyes. Open mouth with four teeth. 1939. $32.00. 12" $32.00. 19" $38.00

26" DREAM BABY. Stuffed cloth body. Composition flange neck, head & limbs. Cry voice. Blue tin sleep eyes. Lightly molded hair. 1935. MARKS: DREAM BABY. $45.00

16" DREAM BABY. All composition. Brown sleep eyes. Deep molded -painted brown hair. Open mouth/two teeth. 1939. MARKS: DREAM BABY, on head. $25.00

22" MY ANGEL. Stuffed cloth body. Latex limbs. Early vinyl head with little girl molded hair (full bangs). Inset blue eyes. Closed mouth. Sold also as Angel Skin Doll. 1948. $25.00

15" NANCY LEE. Vinyl body with stuffed vinyl head and limbs. Glued on wig. Very "high" forehead. Long unusual eyebrows. Large sleep eyes. MARKS: ARRANBEE, on head. $45.00 1951.

15" BABY BUNTING. Latex body & limbs. Vinylite (by Bakelite Co.) head with molded painted hair. Blue sleep eyes. Open/ closed mouth. 1954. MARKS: 17BBS/R&B/D6, on head. $32.00

21" NANETTE. Hard plastic walker body. Stuffed vinyl head. Rooted hair. Sleep eyes. Looks like Alex. Cissy. MARKS: 23 ARV/R&B, on head. 210, on back. 1953. $22.00

23" TAFFY. Hard plastic walker body. Stuffed vinyl head. Rooted hair. Sleep eyes. Same doll as above only marked: R & B, on head. 1954. $22.00

16" ANGEL FACE. All vinyl baby with poodle curled hair. Sleep eyes. Open mouth/nurser. Molded tongue. All fingers open and seperate. MARKS: R & B, on head. 1956. $18.00. 20" $22.00. 25" $26.00. 28" $30.00

36" MY ANGEL WALKING DOLL. Plastic & vinyl. Long rooted hair/full bangs. Sleep blue eyes. Closed smile mouth. 2nd & 3rd fingers curled. MARKS: R & B, on head. $55.00

17" MY ANGEL. All vinyl. Toddler body. Rooted DUTCH BOB hair. Sleep eyes. Closed mouth. 1957. $18.00. 26" has side part hair. $26.00. MARKS: R & B, on head.

35

23" "NANETTE" Cloth body. Composition swivel head on shoulder plate. ¾ composition long straight legs. Open mouth. MARKS: ARRANBEE, on head. 1936. $38.00

18" "DEBU-TEEN" Cloth body. Composition head and limbs. MARKS: R & B, on head. 1940. $40.00

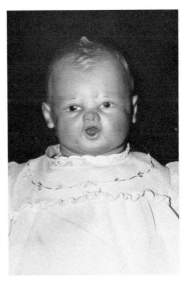

13" "PRINCESS DOLL" Brown tin sleep eyes. All composition. Dress same material as Alexander's "Princess Elizabeth" dolls. MARKS: R & B, on head. TAG: THIS GARMENT/MADE OF/100% ACETATE RAYON. 1941. $30.00

19" "BABY NANCY LEE" Cloth body with vinyl limbs and head. Cryer. Painted blue eyes. Wide spread fingers. MARKS: R & B, on head. Designed by the Sommerman Destry Agency. 1950. $22.00

24" EMMETT KELLY. Stuffed cloth body. Molded vinyl head. Inset glassene eyes. Bald except rooted red hair above ears. TAG: EXCLUSIVE LICENSE/BABY BARRY/TOY N.Y.C./EMMETT KELLY/WILLIE THE CLOWN. $55.00

14" LI'L ABNER. Came with stuffed cloth body and also all vinyl. Molded, painted features. MARKS: 1957/BABY BARRY DOLL/ 25 $45.00. DAISY $45.00. MAMMY $75.00. PAPPY $65.00

21" SAME AS ABOVE. LI'L ABNER $65.00. DAISY $65.00. MAMMY $95.00. PAPPY $85.00

18" SWEETKINS. Latex body. Stuffed vinyl head. FLIRTY blue sleep eyes. Open/closed mouth. Molded-painted hair. 1953. MARKS: BELLE, on head. $22.00

12" MISS B. One piece vinyl body and limbs. Vinyl head with rooted hair. Sleep blue eyes. Closed mouth. MARKS: none. SOME: B/2. 1954. $1.00

18" BALLERINA BELLE. Hard plastic body and legs. Legs in toe dance position & made in one piece. Vinyl arms & head. Arms bent. MARKS: 16-VW, on head. 1956. $3.00

19" SUNSHINE BABY. All vinyl. Molded-painted hair. Hair in point on top of head. Sleep blue eyes. Open/closed mouth -molded tongue. Painted lashes below eyes. MARKS: none. SOME: B-V-4. $12.00

10" BEE BEE. Cloth body. Vinyl head and limbs. Open/closed mouth. Two upper teeth. Seperate finger and toes. Painted lashes below only. MARKS: BELLE, on head. $10.00

12" POOR PITIFUL PEARL. All vinyl. Rooted long blonde hair. Sleep blue eyes. MARKS: A/BROOKGLAD/CREATION, on head. 1957. $20.00

13" POOR PITIFUL PEARL. All vinyl. Rooted long blonde hair. Sleep blue eyes. MARKS: A BROOKGLAD CREATION, on head. 1957. $20.00

17" POOR PITIFUL PEARL. All one piece stuffed vinyl body. Vinyl head. Long blonde rooted hair. Sleep blue eyes. MARKS: GLAD TOY, on head. Large A, on body. 1956. $35.00

17" POOR PITIFUL PEARL. Plastic body & legs. Vinyl arms & head. Rooted blonde hair. Blue sleep eyes. MARKS: 1963/WM STEIG /HORSMAN DOLLS INC. on head. $20.00

20" "ALFRED E. NEWMAN" (Mad Magazine mascot) One piece vinyl body, arms & legs. Vinyl head. Painted features & hair. MARKS: BABY BERRY/1961, on head. 17/V-, on back. $50.00

BELLE
19" "PLAYMATE WALKER" All hard plastic. Glued on wig. Blue sleep eyes. Open mouth/four teeth. Jointed knees. Pin hipped joints. Head turns as walkes. MARKS: none. 1951. $8.00

14" "LAURAL & HARDY" Cloth & vinyl. MARKS: 1973, on feet. TAG: LARRY HARMAN PICTURE CORP/MADE IN HONG KONG. BERMAN & ANDERSON INC. $4.00 each.

BROOKGLAD 18"
"GOLDILOCKS" Sleep blue eyes. All vinyl. MARKS: BROOKGLAD, on head. $22.00

20" BABY BLOSSOM. Composition shoulder head, arms & lower bent legs. Stuffed body & upper legs. Molded blonde hair. Sleep eyes. Closed mouth, dimples. 1928. MARKS: DES & COPY-RIGHT/BY J. L. KALLUS/MADE IN U.S. A. $65.00

16" LITTLE ANNIE ROONEY. All composition with one piece body & head. Painted black eyes to side. Smile mouth. Thin straight legs jointed to sides of hips. 1926. $75.00

12" BETTY BOOP. Composition with joints (ball) at shoulders, elbows, wrists, thighs, knees & ankles. Painted-molded black hair. 1931. Copyright by Kallus MARKS: BETTY BOOP. $65.00

12" & 16" JOY. Wood & composition. Jointed elbows, wrists, knees & ankles. Molded curls with loop for ribbon. Side glance painted eyes. Smile mouth. MARKS: DES. & COPY'T/JOY/J.L.KALLUS. 1932. $65.00 & $75.00

15" SCOOTLES. All composition. Molded-painted hair. Painted eyes. 1930's WHITE: $110.00, BROWN or BLACK: $145.00

16" KEWPIE. All composition. Molded wings on back. Painted eyes to side. Fully jointed. WHITE $55.00. BROWN $75.00. SIGNED ROSE O'NEILL.

12" KEWPIE. All composition. Molded wings, fully jointed. WHITE $45.00. BROWN $65.00. Signed.

12" KEWPIE. All composition. Jointed arms only. Signed. WHITE $45.00. BROWN $65.00

18" CARNIVAL KEWPIE. Chalk. Jointed arms only. On self base. $27.00. 10" $24.00

7" KEWPIE. Talcum powder shaker. Signed Rose O'Neill. $75.00

15" MISS PEEP. Cloth body. Latex limbs. Earliest doll of this line. Inset eyes. Closed mouth. $22.00. Early 1950's.

15" MISS PEEP. Patented jointed arms & legs. Inset eyes. 1969. MARKS: USA53/CAMEO. $18.00

18" BABY MINE. All vinyl with same joints as the Miss Peep. Molded -painted hair. Blue sleep eyes/lashes. Open/closed mouth. 1962. MARKS: CAMEO, on head & body. $55.00. PAINTED EYE VERSION: $75.00

"HOHO" White plaster. Original mold. MARKS: ROSE O'NEILL /1940/COPYRIGHT. $30.00

24" "DYP-A-BABE" 1956. Head used as AFFECTIONATELY PEANUT 1958 and PLUM in 1952. One piece laytex with vinyl head. MARKS: CAMEO, on head. $40.00

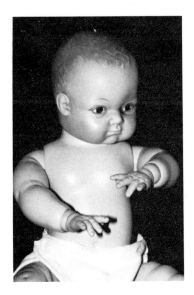

18" "BABY" Plastic body with vinyl head, legs and hands. Jointed wrists. Doll is strung. MARKS: CAMEO, on body. CAMEO C JLK/2, on head. $22.00

12" "PETE THE PUP" Composition and wood. Ca. 1933. $65.00

30" LENCI. Long legged bed doll. Cut out felt clothes. Large floppy hat. $165.00

16" LENCI. Little girl type. Felt clothes, various designs. $85.00

16" LENCI. Little boy type. Felt clothes, various designs. $95.00

17" FOOTBALL PLAYER. All cloth with yarn hair. Felt ears. Removable top & helmet. MARKS: TRADITIONAL/KRUGER/ N.Y.C. $7.00

15" LITTLE LULU. All cloth. Molded painted features. Sewn on shoes & socks. String hair. $35.00. In western clothes. $55.00. 1959.

18" LITTLE ORPHAN ANNIE. All cloth. Buckram face mask. Red brownish mohair wig. Seperate dress marked ORPHAN ANNIE. Tag on doll: SATURDAY EVENING POST. $85.00

19" ARCHIE. All lithographed. Orange hair, red shirt. Orange & black striped bell bottom pants. MARKS: ARCHIE, on shirt front. $10.00

17" LITTLE ORPHAN ANNIE. All cloth. Litho features. Large round eyes with no pupils. Red yarn hair. Red dress with black belt. 1967. TAG: 1967/REMCO IN. INC. $10.00

20" NANCY. All litho. cloth. Plush hair. Sewn on shoes & socks. Tag on front: NANCY/1972 UNITED/FEATURE SYNDICATE INC. Made by STACEY LEE ORIGINALS. $16.00

40" SISTER PAT. 1949. All cloth with buckram face mask. Painted features. Eyes to side. Dressed in short sleeve shirt and flaired legged long pants. MARKS: M & S DOLL CO. $12.00

18" LITTLE AUDREY. Cloth with vinyl head. Molded red hair. Painted features. TAG: LITTLE AUDREY/HARVEY FAMOUS CARTOONS. $25.00

23" ELOISE. Cloth with plastic face mask. Painted features. Eyes to side. Yellow yarn hair. TAG: ELOISE/ELOISE LTD./ HOLLYTOY CO. N. Y. 1958. $22.00

10" TATTERS. All cloth with yellow yarn hair. Button eyes with felt lids. Painted features. Rag in tatters clothes. Pull string talker. TAG: TATTERS/1964 MATTEL INC. $15.00

17" HANSEL. Wool dust filled, cloth covered body. Sewn on clothes. Painted features. Blonde mohair sewn on wig. TAG: HANSEL /RAG DOLL/KNICKERBACHER TOY CO. 1969. $2.00

18" "RAG MOP" All cloth with yarn hair. Original. Removable clothes. MARKS: none. 1967. $3.00

15" "HUGGLES" Cloth with yarn hair. Felt eyes and nose. Printed mouth. TAG: ANOTHER HUGGLES/BY/FUN WORLD 1968. $2.00

9" "PAUL BUNYAN" All cloth & felt. Painted features. Original but had woodsmen ax. PAPER TAG: 1342 PAUL BUNYAN/ DREAM DOLLS. CLOTH TAG: DREAM DOLLS/R. DAKIN & CO. 1969. $4.00

10" "SCOOBY DOO". Cloth with felt eyes and yarn nose. MARKS: TAG: 1970 HANNA BARBERA PROD. OTHER SIDE: AS SEEN ON T.V./I.S. SUTTON & SONS, Inc. $6.00

DELUXE READING & DELUXE TOPPER are the same company.

20" TICKLES. Plastic & vinyl. Battery operated. Doll cries, laughs when tickled or spanked. MARKS: 1963/DELUXE READING /75. $8.00

14" BABY BRITE. Plastic & vinyl. Battery operated. Push button and doll turns head and sleeps when laying down. Other button: pushes arms up to be picked up. MARKS: 15/DELUXE READING CORP./1963 15MENO.H. $10.00

21" NANCY NURSE. Plastic & vinyl. Battery operated. Talker: "I feel sick" etc. MARKS: 6/1963/DELUXE READING. $7.00

21" BABY BOO. Plastic & vinyl. Battery operated. Doll stops crying when covered with a blanket, hugged or given a pacifier. MARKS: 111/DELUXE READING CO./1965. $8.00

18" BABY MAGIC. Plastic & vinyl. Blue sleep eyes with discs in place of tear ducts. Comes with Magic Wand that opens and closes the eyes. MARKS: DELUXE READING CORP./1966. $12.00

21" SUSY HOMEMAKER. Plastic & vinyl. Swivel neck. Jointed knees. Came with many appliances. Open/closed mouth smile. MARKS: K21/DELUXE READING CORP./1966, $10.00. Closed mouth version. $6.00

18" LITTLE MISS FUSSY. Plastic & vinyl. Battery operated. Drinks from bottle, wets then fuss until diaper is changed. MARKS: K7/DELUXE TOPPER/1967. $6.00

19" BABY CATCH A BALL. Plastic and vinyl with wrist metal balls (bracelets) to allow doll to catch special tin ball. Doll returns ball. MARKS: 2871/17EYE/PB2/75/DELUXE TOPPER/1968. $12.00

18" BABY PEEP N PLAY. Plastic & vinyl. Battery operated. Raises hands to cover eyes, plays accordion, picks up bottle and drinks. MARKS: 72/DELUXE TOPPER/1968. $9.00

10" BABY PARTY. Plastic & vinyl. Battery operated. Blows up balloon, blows whistle and blows out candles. MARKS: 2770 /17 EYE 39/DELUXE TOPPER. 1968. $12.00. 18" $8.00

18" LUV N CARE. Plastic & vinyl. Battery operated. Red light behind face glows to show fever, try to feed doll & she rubs tummy. Take temperature and give her a "pill" and she stops crying. MARKS: DELUXE TOPPER. 1969. $14.00

11" "BUSY BABY WALKER"
Plastic body, legs with molded on
shoes. Vinyl arms and head with
rooted white hair. Painted blue
eyes. Battery operated walker.
MARKS: 2855/NEW/DELUXE
TOPPER/1968. $5.00

6" "DAWN" An original dress.
"Starlight Ball" no. 0812.1971.
$4.00

6" "DAWN AND HER MUSIC
BOX". Box marked both Topper
Toys and Mfg. by IRWIN TOY
LTD. (CANADA) Box and ins-
tructions are in English and French.
Key wind. DAWN'S HEAD IS
MARKED: P11A. 1971. $9.00

6" "DENISE" model from Dawn
series. Came in two different
"original" dresses. 1971. $8.00

9" MICKEY MOUSE. Molded and painted composition head. Wooden body. MARKS: WALT DISNEY, on back. KNICKERBOCKER/TOY/CO. N.Y.C., lower back. $55.00

9" PINOCCHIO. All composition with limbs shaped to look like wood. Jointed only at shoulders. Molded-painted clothes MARKS: PINOCCHIO/MADE IN U.S.A./W.Disney Prod./C. T. $55.00

12" DWARFS. Composition heads. All cloth bodies with black felt shoes as part of bodies. Deeply molded-painted features. MARKS: ALEXANDER ON BACK AND TAG. $45.00 each. $350.00 for set.

11" MINNIE MOUSE. Molded-painted rubber. Painted panties with removable red/white polka dot sundress. MARKS: WALT DISNEY PRODUCTIONS/THE SUN RUBBER CO./BARBERTON O. U.S.A. $12.00

4" BIG BAD WOLF. Molded-painted bisque. Orange pants, green suspenders & red hat. Both arms molded to body. MARKS: WALT DISNEY/MADE IN JAPAN, on back. $14.00

19" CHRISTOPHER ROBIN. Cloth body. Molded-painted vinyl head with painted blue eyes. Watermelon smile mouth. MARKS: TAG: WALT DISNEY/CHARACTER/COPYRIGHT WALT DISNEY PRODUCTIONS/J. SWEDLIN INC. LICENSEE. $45.00

10" MICKEY MOUSE. All vinyl with molded on panties. Jointed head only. MARKS: WALT DISNEY PROD./SUN RUBBER CO. 1957. $10.00

12" MOUSEKETEER GIRL. Molded on short jumpsuit with imprint of M.Mouse head on front. Jointed neck, shoulders & hips. Molded on cap. MARKS: WALT DISNEY PROD./SUN RUBBER CO. 1958. $10.00

15" PANCHITO. Felt & velvet body over stuffed wired armature. Felt eyes. Open/closed beak. TAG: WALT DISNEY PROD. /CHARACTER NOVELTY CO./LICENSEE. SOUTH NORWALK, CONN. $16.00

4" JIMINY CRICKET. Cloth body and limbs. Composition head with painted features. MARKS: JIMINY CRICKET/W.D.PR. KN.T.Co./U.S.A., on head. $14.00

12" STEPMOTHER. Stuffed cloth body. Composition head and limbs. Gray mohair wig. Painted mouth/one tooth. MARKS: WALT DISNEY'S MARIONETTES/"STEPMOTHER"/ (DISGUISED)/MADAME ALEXANDER N.Y.U.S.A. $55.00

45

12" "BASHFUL DWARF" All composition. Fully jointed. Painted features. 1937. $45.00

12" "SOLDIERS FROM BABE IN TOYLAND". Vinyl heads. Original. TAGS, on bottom of feet: LINE/MAR/TOYS, in circle. /JAPAN/LINEMAR CO. INC./1961/WALT DISNEY PRODUCTIONS. $12.00

18" "PLUTO" All foam over wire. Painted features. MARKS: BENDY, on back on collar. 1965. $6.00

8" "SMALL WORLD OF DOLLS" All vinyl. Painted features. MARKS: PRESSMAN TOYS/WALT DISNEY /PROD. 1965. Designed by Walt Disney and came in a "round the world" series. $5.00

18" MISS CHARMING. Shirley Temple look-a-like. All composition. Blonde mohair. Blue tin sleep eyes. Open mouth/six teeth. MARKS: E.G., on head. $35.00

15" CHRISTIE BRIDE. All composition. Mohair wig. Sleep blue eyes. Rosebud mouth. MARKS: E. GOLDBERGER, on head. $22.00. 19" $32.00

12" TWIN. All vinyl. Molded-painted light brown hair. Closed eyes. Open/closed yawning mouth with one molded tooth. MARKS: Y2/EEGEE, on head. $18.00

20" ROGER. Stuffed pink cloth body. Stuffed soft vinyl head & limbs. Blue sleep eyes. Closed mouth. Deep molded brown hair in swirl curl in middle of forehead. 1955. MARKS: EEGEE/20, on head. $40.00

21" KARENA BALLERINA. Hard plastic with vinyl head. Rooted hair. Sleep eyes. Jointed knees and ankles. Walker, head turns. MARKS: EEGEE, on head. 1958. $16.00

13" MISS PRIMM. All cotton stuffed vinyl. One piece body & limbs. Sleep eyes. Small rosebud type mouth. MARKS: EEGEE/10/P, on head. $10.00

18" MISS PRIMM. Hard plastic body & limbs. Jointed elbows & knees. Walker, head turns. Dutch bob hair with full bangs. Closed rosebud mouth. $20.00. 20" $22.00

36" ANNETTE. Rigid vinyl body & limbs. Walker legs. Vinyl head. Came with long blonde hair with full bangs and curly hair. Sleep eyes. Closed mouth. MARKS: EEGEE. $65.00

19" SUSAN STROLLER. Hard plastic body & legs. Vinyl arms & head. Jointed above elbows. Jointed knees. Open grill work in stomach. MARKS: EEGEE, on head. $32.00

26" SUSAN STROLLER. Hard plastic body and limbs. Jointed knees only. Open/closed mouth. Sleep eyes. Rooted saran hair with full bangs. MARKS: EEGEE, $45.00

14" PATTICAKE. Stuffed cloth body. Vinyl head and curved limbs. Rooted pixie cut hair. Sleep blue eyes. Press stomach and arms move to clap hands & doll gurgles. MARKS: EEGEE/10, on head. 1963. $15.00. 20" $22.00

14" PRINCESS BOUDOIR DOLL. All vinyl, fully jointed. Pastel rooted hair. Sleep eyes. Nylon dress with ruffles over a rayon covered wire hoop. MARKS: EEGEE. 1963. $12.00

13" "BOBBY" All vinyl. Deeply molded hair. Inset blue eyes. Open/closed mouth. Dimpled cheeks. MARKS: EEGEE, on head. 1955. $25.00

20" "CUDDLE-BUN" One piece body, arms and legs. Legs are wired to be posable. Molded hair. Molded brows. Sleep blue eyes. Original dress. 1956. MARKS: EEGEE/ VS-20/15, on back. EEGEE, on head. V, on lower back. $9.00

28" "ANNETTE" Plastic with vinyl arms and head. Sleep blue eyes. MARKS: EEGEE/1961, on head. $22.00

13" "CANDY" Vinyl with rooted blonde hair. Blue sleep eyes/lashes. Toddler body. MARKS: EEGEE on head. 1963. $8.00

16" CAMILLA. Wired foam body and limbs. Gauntlet vinyl hands. Vinyl head with sleep eyes. Open/closed mouth. Rooted hair. MARKS: EEGEE 16, on head. $8.00

15" BABETTE. Cloth stuffed baby body, Stuffed vinyl arms and legs. Toddler fat legs. Painted eyes. Twin ponytails. $6.00. 25" with sleep eyes. $18.00

18" PUPPETRINA. Baby doll with vinyl arms, legs & head. Rooted blonde hair. Blue sleep eyes. Open/closed mouth. Cloth body with insertion for hand to operate her. MARKS: EEGEE, on head. $7.00

13" I'M HUNGRY. Molded light brown hair with locks far down on forehead. Painted side glancing blue eyes. Open mouth/nurser. Full jointed vinyl. MARKS: EEGEE, on head 1962. $6.00

14" BABY TANDY TALKS. Cotton & foam stuffed body. Vinyl head and limbs. Sleep eyes. Open closed mouth. Pull string operated talker. 1963. $18.00

22" PUPPETRINA. Cloth body with puppet pocket inside. Vinyl head with large sleep eyes. Open/closed mouth/painted teeth. Long thin straight legs. MARKS: 1963/EEGEE CO./PAT. PEND. on head. $35.00

21" CHARMER GEMETTE. All vinyl. Fully jointed. Blue sleep eyes. closed mouth. Adult figure. MARKS: 8/EEGEE CO./1963/10 on head. $8.00

14" BABY LUV. Cotton stuffed pink floppy baby body, with panties as part of the body. Vinyl arms, legs and head. Open/closed mouth. Painted eyes with star shaped highlights. . MARKS: 14 B.T./EEGEE CO., on head. $28.00

14" MISS DEBBY. All one piece vinyl body & limbs. Vinyl head. Very large sleep blue eyes. MARKS: 1½-H/EEGEE, on head. EEGEE/15H on back. $6.00

20" TERRY TALKS. Plastic and vinyl. Rooted hair. Sleep eyes. Battery operated talker. MARKS: 19U/EEGEE CO/3, on head. 1965. $6.00

14" PLAYPEN BABY. Plastic and vinyl. Blue sleep eyes. Open mouth /nurser with hole in roof of the mouth. MARKS: 13/14AA/ EEGEE CO. 1968. $3.00

17" MISS SUNBEAM. Plastic and vinyl with rooted yellow hair. Blue sleep eyes. Open/closed mouth with molded & painted teeth. Dimples. MARKS: EEGEE, on head. $10.00

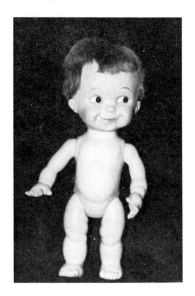

12" "STONEAGE BABY" Plastic body. Vinyl arms, legs & head. Red rooted hair. Black plastic balls for eyes. Excellent modeling around mouth. MARKS: EEGEE, on head. 1963. $4.00

18" "LOVELY LISA BRIDE" Using the "Gemmette" body. Sleep blue eyes. Original. MARKS: none. 1963. $5.00

16½" "FLOWERKIN & also SANDY in 1966. Plastic & vinyl. To side black eyes. MARKS: FI /EEGEE, on head. GOLDBERGER /MFG. CO. INC/PAT. PEND, on back. $9.00

22" "CAROL" Plastic body and legs. Vinyl head & arms. Sleep green eyes/lashes. Smiling. Plastic tabs in back of ears. Neck seated into body. Nice modeled hands. MARKS: EEGEE CO./15 PM, on head. 1969. $6.00

18" ROSEMARY. Composition shoulder head and limbs. Stuffed cloth body. Blue tin sleep eyes. Open mouth. MARKS: EFF-ANBEE/ROSEMARY/WALK TALK SLEEP/MADE IN U.S.A. $45.00

22" MARILEE. Composition shoulder head and limbs. Brown sleep eyes. Open mouth/teeth. MARKS: EFFANBEE/MARILEE/COPYR./DOLL. $40.00

14" PAT-O-PAT. Composition swivel head. Stuffed cloth body. Gauntlet compo. hands. Painted features. Press mechanism in body & hands clap together. MARKS: EFFANBEE/MADE IN U.S.A., on head. $40.00

12" BYE-LO TYPE. Cloth body & legs. Celluloid hands. Composition head. Painted hair. Blue sleep eyes. Closed mouth. MARKS: EFFANBEE, on head. $65.00

26" KALI-KO-KATE. All percale cloth stuffed with body & clothes from same material (checkered). Seperate thumbs. Flat, hand painted face. MARKS: EFFANBEE/U.S.A. $45.00

6" WEE PATSY. All composition with one piece body & head. Painted on shoes/socks. Painted features & molded head band. MARKS: EFFANBEE/WEE PATSY. $85.00

7" BABY TINYETTE. (Called PATSY TINYETTE). All compo. with jointed neck, arms & legs. Very bent arms & legs. Painted features & hair. MARKS: EFFANBEE/BABY TINYETTE. $50.00

8" BABY TINYETTE. Same as above but with straight legs. $50.00

8" PATSY BABYETTE. All composition with slightly bent arms & legs. Sleep eyes. Reddish brown molded hair. $50.00

9" PATSY BABYETTE. All composition with slightly bent arms & legs. Sleep eyes. Fur wig over unpainted molded hair. BOTH MARKED: EFFANBEE/PATSY BABYETTE. $50.00

9" PATSYETTE. All compo. Little girl with jointed limbs. Right arm in bent position. Brown painted eyes, molded hair (no band) MARKS: EFFANBEE/PATSYETTE/DOLL. $35.00

9" PATSYETTE. All compo. Molded black hair. MARKS: SAME. $60.00

9" PATSYETTE. All compo. Blonde mohair wig over unpainted molded hair. MARKS: SAME $40.00

16" "BABY BUBBLES" (NEGRO)
Fat cloth body. All composition
bent legs. Composition arms. Brown
tin sleep eyes. 1926 into 1930's.
$95.00

20" All composition. Sleep blue
eyes. MARKS: PETITE, on head
and body. 1935. $35.00

16" "DEEWEES COCHRAN".
MARKS: EFFANBEE/ANNE
SHIRLEY, on back. All compo
sition. Open mouth/teeth. Called
"Ice Queen" but came dressed in
many ways. Original dress. 1937.
$85.00

14" "ANNE SHIRLEY" All composition. MARKS: EFFANBEE/
ANNE SHIRLEY, on back. 1939.
$50.00

EFFANBEE

11" BABY BUBBLES. Rubber body & limbs with palms down. Composition head with open mouth/two teeth up and down. Sleep brown eyes. Molded hair. MARKS: BABY BUBBLES/ EFFANBEE. $35.00. 14" $40.00. 16" $45.00. 18" $50.00

10" PATSY BABY. All composition. Both arms bend, very curved baby legs. Sleep eyes. Molded curly hair. MARKS: EFFANBEE PATSY BABY, head & body. $45.00

10" PATSY BABY. All compo. Same as above but with painted eyes. $45.00

10" PATSY BABY. All compo. Negro. Three yarns tuffs of hair. MARKS: SAME. $65.00

13" PATSY BABY. Cloth body. Compo. gauntlet hands. Compo. head attached with wooden plug. Sleep eyes, brown molded curly hair. MARKS: EFFANBEE on head. $65.00

11" PATSY JR. All compo. Full joints. Right arm bent. Molded red hair. Painted brown eyes. Head band. MARKS: EFFANBEE /PATSY JR./DOLL. (Referred to as PATSYKINS) $40.00

11" PATSY JR. Same as above but with sleep eyes and mohair wig over unpainted molded hair. $45.00

14" PATSY. One piece compo. head & shoulderplate. Cloth body. Compo. arms slightly bent. Compo. legs. MARKS: EFFANBEE /PATSY/COPYR./DOLL. Came with both painted & sleep eyes. Open & closed mouth. $75.00

14" PATSY. All compo. Right arm very bent. Red molded hair/head band. Blue or green painted eyes. MARKS: EFFANBEE/PATSY /DOLL. SOME: SAME but with PAT. PEND. $35.00

14" PATSY. Same as above but with light brown molded hair and NO HEAD BAND. $35.00

14" PATSY. Same as above but with sleep eyes and molded red hair. $50.00

14" PATSY. Same as above but with sleep eyes and mohair/human hair over unpainted molded hair. $60.00

14" PATSY. Same as above but with painted eyes and DARK SKIN TONES. $65.00

14½"PATRICIA. All composition with both arms slightly curved. Straight legs. Sleep eyes. Mohair wig. MARKS: EFFANBEE /PATRICIA. $45.00 In any size other than 14½" $65.00.

14" "HISTORICAL DOLL-1872" Hair designed by Meyer Jacoby. All Composition. Blue decal eyes. Original. 1939. One of a series. $110.00

22" "PATRICIA WALKER" All hard plastic. Walker, head turns. Original. MARKS: EFFANBEE, on head. 1955. $18.00

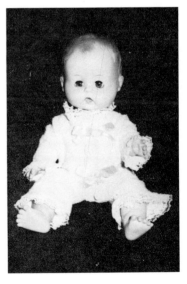

31" "MARY JANE" Plastic & vinyl. Walker. Flirty eyes. Freckles. MARKS: EFFANBEE/MARY JANE. 1962. $30.00

11" "TWINKIE" All vinyl with molded, painted light brown hair. Blue sleep eyes/lashes. Open mouth /nurser. Open hands with palms toward body. Individual toes. MARKS: EFFANBEE/1963 on head. $4.00

14" SKIPPY. All compo. on a Patsy (marked) body. Molded hair with one long lock down forehead. Painted side glance eyes. MARKS: EFFANBEE/SKIPPY/P.L.CROSBY. $55.00

14" SKIPPY. Cloth body. Compo. head and limbs. Painted black legs. (WORE MILITARY COSTUMES). $65.00. Unpainted legs attached at hips. $65.00

16" PATSY JOAN. All compo. Right arm bent. Molded red hair (no band). Sleep eyes. MARKS: EFFANBEE/PATSY JOAN. $45.00

19" PATSY ANN. All compo. Bent right arm. Sleep eyes. Molded red hair (no band). MARKS: EFFANBEE/PATSY ANN/PAT. no.1283558. $50.00

19" PATSY ANN. Same as above but with wigs over unpainted molded hair, or an open mouth/teeth, or dark skinned, or with brown sleep eyes. $60.00

22" PATSY LOU. All compo. Bent right arm. Red molded hair (no band). Closed mouth, green eyes. MARKS: EFFANBEE /PATSY LOU. $125.00

22" PATSY LOU. With brown sleep eyes & open mouth/wig over unpainted molded hair. $125.00. Same but with closed mouth (wigged). $125.00

27" PATSY RUTH. All composition or a cloth body. (Shoulder head with marked LOVUMS Shoulder plate). Both arms slightly curved. Straight legs. Human/mohair wigs. Small "rosebud" closed mouth. MARKS: EFFANBEE/PATSY RUTH. $150.00

30" PATSY MAE. Compo. swivel head on (LOVUMS) shoulder plate. Cloth body. Green sleep eyes. Closed mouth. Wig over unmolded head. Also with brown sleep eyes & open mouth/teeth. MARKS: EFFANBEE/PATSY MAE. $150.00

21" SUGAR BABY. Cloth body. Composition head & limbs. Deeply molded-painted brown hair. Brown sleep eyes. Full closed mouth. MARKS: EFFANBEE/SUGAR BABY/TRADEMARK. $35.00

18" MISS CHIPS. All vinyl. Large sleep eyes. Rooted dark hair. MARKS: EFFANBEE/1965/1700, on head. $22.00

21" BETTINA. Cloth body. Vinyl head & limbs. Sleep eyes. Rooted hair. Open/closed mouth. MARKS: EFFANBEE/1967. Also called PRECIOUS BABY: $18.00

12" BABY BUTTERBALL. All vinyl. Blue sleep eyes. Open mouth /nurser. MARKS: EFFANBEE/1969/8569. $5.00

18" "BETTINA" Plastic and vinyl. Sleep blue eyes/lashes. Same body as Susie Sunshine. Since she did not sell as Susie Sunshine, was put out year later as "Bettina". MARKS: EFFANBEE/1964. Original. $20.00

15" All vinyl with rooted blonde hair. Blue sleep eyes. Deep molded open mouth/nurser. Dimples. MARKS: EFFANBEE/1964, on back. EFFANBEE/1965/2500U, on head. $4.00

18" "SWEETIE PIE" Cloth body with vinyl head, arms and legs. Rooted blonde hair. Blue sleep eyes/lashes. MARKS: 17/EFFANBEE/1969/9660, on head. $6.00

8" "GIRL SCOUT" All vinyl. Brown sleep eyes. MARKS: EFFANBEE/FLUFFY, on head. Original. 1969. $6.00

13" BUBBLES. Cloth body and legs. Composition arms and head. Molded-painted hair. Sleep eyes. Open/closed mouth/two painted upper teeth. MARKS: EFFANBEE/BUBBLES. $45.00. Colored $110.00

17" HEART BEAT LOVUMS. Composition shoulder head and limbs. Cloth body. Open mouth. Molded hair. Wind up heart beats. MARKS: EFFANBEE/LOVUMS/PAT. No. 1283, 5558. $55.00

12½" BABYETTE. Cloth body. Composition limbs & head. Painted closed eyes. Dark painted hair. MARKS: F & B/BABYETTE. $35.00

11" SUZETTE. All composition. Full joints. Painted brown eyes (also sleep brown eyes). MARKS: SUZETTE/EFFANBEE/USA, on head. SUZETTE/EFFANBEE/MADE IN U.S.A. on back. $35.00

22" LITTLE LADY. All composition. Both painted and sleep eyes. Human as well as human hair wigs. Some floss wigs. MARKS: EFFANBEE/ANNE SHIRLEY. $65.00

21" COLORED LITTLE LADY. Same as above and marked the same. $85.00

21" AMERICAN CHILDREN. All composition. Human hair wigs. Painted eyes. Closed mouths, MARKS: EFFANBEE/ANNE SHIRLEY. $110.00

21" AMERICAN CHILDREN. All composition. Painted eyes. Human hair wigs. MARKS: EFFANBEE/AMERICAN CHILDREN, on head. EFFANBEE/ANNE SHIRLEY, on back. $125.00

14" LUCIFER. Wood & string marionette body. Compo. hands, feet & head. Molded painted features. This is a Negro boy. MARKS: LUCIFER/V. AUSTIN/EFFANBEE. $35.00

14" CLIPPO THE CLOWN. Wood & string marionette body. Composition arms, legs and head. Molded-painted features. MARKS: EFFANBEE/V. AUSTIN. $35.00

19" HONEY WALKER. All hard plastic. Walker, head turns. Glued on wig. Sleep eyes. Closed mouth. MARKS: EFFANBEE, on head. $35.00

11" MICKEY. All vinyl. Painted eyes. Freckles. Came dressed in many different boys outfits. Many have molded on hats. $5.00

16" LIL SWEETIE. All vinyl. Sleep eyes with no lashes and has no brows. Open mouth/nurser. MARKS: 5667/EFFANBEE/1967, on head. EFFANBEE/1967, on back. $10.00

8" "CAMPFIRE" All vinyl. Sleep blue eyes. MARKS: EFFANBEE /FLUFFY, on head. 1969. $6.00

8½" "FLUFFY" All vinyl with sleep eyes. Dressed in Bluebird uniform. MARKS: EFFANBEE 1965. 1969. $6.00

11" "HALF PINT" The EFFAN-BEE FAN CLUB mascot. Tag made out by fan club: OFFICIAL CLUB DOLL NO.1/JANUARY 1974. $12.00

13" "BLACK CANDY KID" All composition. Original. Leather boxing gloves. Sleep brown eyes. Has "Champ" written across back of robe. 1944. $65.00

11½" ESKIMO BOY. Full jointed vinyl. Rooted black hair. Side glance bead eyes. Comes in Eskimo suit and Indian suit. MARKS: REGAL/MADE IN CANADA. $5.00

10" ESKIMO. Plastic and vinyl. Black hair. Painted black eyes. Dressed both as an Eskimo and Indian. MARKS: REGAL TOY/ MADE IN CANADA. $3.00

12" INDIAN GIRL. Full jointed vinyl. Rooted long black hair. Side glance bead eyes. MARKS: REGAL/CANADA. $4.00

12" SEXED BABIES. Full jointed vinyl. Blue & brown sleep eyes. MARKS: 2939/10EYE/REGAL TOY LTD./MADE IN CANADA /129G. 1967. $25.00. 16" MARKS: 2739/14EYE REGAL TOY LTD./MADE IN CANADA. $45.00

12½" INDIAN GIRL. All composition. Full joints. Mohair wig. Painted black eyes. Closed mouth. MARKS: RELIABLE/MADE IN/ CANADA. $25.00

16" MOUNTY POLICEMAN. Stuffed body & legs. Composition head and arms. Portrait type head with painted features. MARKS: R.C.M.P., on uniform. RELIABLE/MADE IN CANADA, on head. $65.00

14" CANADIAN DIONNE QUINT. All full jointed composition. Brown sleep eyes. Toddler legs. Came in pastel dresses. MARKS: RELIABLE/MADE IN CANADA. $28.00

18" NURSE (RED CROSS). Excelsior stuffed body & upper limbs. Composition head and lower limbs. Straight legs. Painted blue eyes. 1944. MARKS: A/RELIABLE/DOLL/MADE IN CANADA. $25.00

20" NEW WETUMS. Plastic body. Vinyl arms legs and head. Palms down & curved baby legs. Side glancing painted eyes. Open mouth/nurser. MARKS: RELIABLE (in script)/Canada. $12.00

18" DRINK BABY. From Horsman's Thirstie Line molds. Full jointed vinyl. Arms & legs bent. Sleep eyes. Painted hair. Full open/nurser mouth. MARKS: RELIABLE/CANADA, in a square. $6.00

16" SUSAN. All vinyl. Fully jointed. Blue sleep eyes. Bent baby legs. Open/nurser mouth. MARKS: RELIABLE/MADE IN CANADA, in square on head. RELIABLE, in script in an oval/CANADA, on back. 1964. $5.00

15" DOCTOR & MOUNTIE. Hard plastic body and limbs. Vinyl head with deep molded side part black hair. Oval sleep eyes. Open/ closed mouth. 1955. MARKS: DEEANCEE, on head. $22.00

12" Fully jointed plastic. Sculptured eyes. 1965. TAG: MONAFON/MADE IN AUSTRIA. $3.00

8½" "CLAUDINE PETIT" All plastic with vinyl head. Sleep brown eyes/lashes. Reddish brown hair. MARKS: S 8 D/MADE IN FRANCE, on back. $8.00

6" "PLAYMATE" All early vinyl. Painted blue eyes. Jointed neck, shoulders and hips. Painted on black strap shoes & white socks. Original. MARKS: ARI, in a tri-angle./GERMANY. $3.00

9" "GURA" All plastic with painted eyes. Original. MARKS: TAG: "GURA", BOX: GURA/ BAD TOLLY/BAVARIA/58./ MADE IN WEST GERMANY. GURA, on head and body.

$6.00

21" ROSLEE. Rigid plastic & vinyl. Pull string talker. Sleep eyes. Closed mouth with two molded-painted upper teeth. MARKS: ROSEBUD, on head. ROSEBUD MATTEL/MADE IN ENGLAND, on body. $16.00

6" TEENIE. All jointed hard plastic. Both arms bent. Molded hair. Sleep eyes. Closed mouth. Slightly bent baby legs. MARKS: ROSEBUD/MADE IN/ENGLAND. $4.00

10" WHIPPER. All full jointed hard plastic. Painted brown hair. Blue sleep eyes. Closed mouth. MARKS: RODEBUD/MADE IN ENGLAND/PAT. NO. 667906. $8.00

20" LITTLE BROTHER. Fully jointed vinyl (Polyflex). Rooted brown hair. Sleep blue eyes. Open/closed mouth. Sexed. 1967. MARKS: MADE IN FRANCE/LAVABLE GRANT TEINT. $65.00

20" LITTLE SISTER. Fully jointed vinyl (Polyflex) rooted blonde hair. Sleep blue eyes. Sexed. 1967. MARKS: MADE IN FRANCE. $65.00

16" DEMIFLEX BABY. Full jointed vinyl. (has yellowish look). Molded-painted hair. Pale blue eyes. Open mouth/nurser. MARKS: TURTLEMARK/SCHILDKROT/GERMANY/40, on head. WASSERDICHT/WATTERPROOF, on back. $22.00

18" NINA. Elastic strung vinyl body & limbs. Vinyl head with rooted blonde hair. Sleep blue eyes. Open/closed mouth with molded teeth. MARKS: 40/42/MADE IN/W. GERMANY. $12.00

27" TOXI. All hard plastic. Pale sleep blue eyes. Open crown/wig. Closed mouth. MARKS. 3 "m"s/70, on head. 3 "m"s/603172 on back. $25.00

11½"LILLI. Prototype of Mattel Barbie. Molded on shoes with holes for stand. MARKS: NONE ON DOLL. STAND: LILLI and MADE IN WESTERN GERMANY. $50.00

7" SWEETHEART. Rigid plastic body & legs. Vinyl arms and head. Blonde hair, painted eyes. Painted on shoes. Key wind. MARKS: SWEETHEART/DANCING DOLL/GERMANY, on head. $6.00

10" BENDABLES. All solid vinyl with painted features and clothes. MARKS: SCHLEICH'S BIEBEFGUREN, on one foot. MADE IN WEST GERMANY/J.N.U.AUSLPAT, on other. Came as various figures. $4.00

15" SEXED BOY & GIRL. Fully jointed vinyl. Rooted hair. Sleep eyes/long lashes. Open/closed mouths. MARKS: MADE IN ITALY, on head. PATTI/MADE IN ITALY, on back $45.00 each.

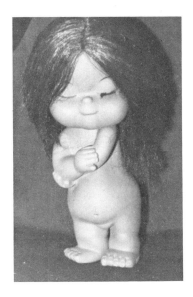

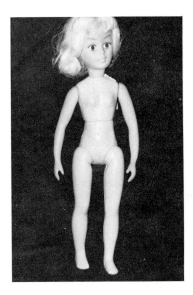

9" All vinyl with rooted black hair. MARKS: HONG KONG, on head. 1971. Same head used on several different body styles. $2.00

13" "MARY ROSE" Jointed waist. White rooted hair. Brown painted eyes. Flat feet. MARKS: MADE IN/HONG KONG. $4.00

11½" "CINDELLA" Plastic and vinyl. Rooted reddish hair, with one section very long. Blue sleep eyes. MARKS: IC, in a square /1967, on head. Made by Italo-cremona. $6.00

9" "MILANO" Brown hair and turned head. Jointed shoulders and hips. MARKS: TAG: MADE IN ITALY. $3.00

ITALY

FOREIGN

20" MY BABY. Latex body with early vinyl head. Deep molded brown hair. Sleep eyes. Open/closed mouth with two upper teeth. 1953. MARKS: N. FARRARI/MY BABY. $45.00

8½" THERSA. Full jointed vinyl. Rooted short blonde hair. Sleep eyes. Open/closed mouth. MARKS: FRANKA, on head. $5.00

10" MINSTREL. Tightly stuffed body and limbs. Face mask with painted features. Mohair wig. Felt clothes. MARKS: GALAFE /MADE IN ITALY & MADE EXPRESSLY FOR A. HARRIS & CO. $5.00

3" MYSTERIOUS DANCING DOLL. Celluloid arms & head. Wire forms body. Arms jointed. MARKS: JAPAN, on top of body. $3.00

10" CRIB MATE. All one piece soft vinyl body, arms & legs. Vinyl head with painted features and molded brown hair (boy), MARKS: JAPAN/1 CWAL, on head. JAPAN on back $3.00

3½" Painted bisque. Jointed shoulders & hips. Slightly bent baby legs. Painted blue eyes. Molded curls. MARKS: MADE IN/OCCUPIED /JAPAN. $6.00

5" All soft molded vinyl. Wings on back. Painted features. Molded top knot hair. Jointed shoulders only. MARKS: JAPAN, on back. Some JAPAN on left arm. $4.00

5" HAWAIIAN. All brown vinyl, jointed at neck only. In kneeling position with arms in front of chest. Rooted hair. Painted features. MARKS: STYLED BY/FORSAM/MADE IN JAPAN. $3.00

5" PEANUT BABY. Jointed celluloid with painted red hair & blue eyes. Bent baby legs. Cardboard peanut "bed". MARKS: WV, on heart, MADE IN JAPAN, on back. PATENT NO. 27636 MADE IN JAPAN, on shell. $12.00

12" PLUM. All celluloid with jointed shoulders & hips. Molded on red "pajama" suit that includes bonnet. One curl on forehead. Painted blue eyes. Closed mouth. Bent baby legs. Also "ORAN- GE", "APPLE" & "BANANA". MARKS: MADE IN/OCCUPIED/ JAPAN. $15.00

6½" All celluloid jointed only at shoulders. Deeply molded, painted hair. Painted blue eyes. Closed watermelon smile mouth. MARKS: a Fleur-de-lis with J in center/MADE IN/OCCUPIED JAPAN. $8.00

12" NINA. All celluloid with molded brown hair. Ribbon glued to hair. Painted blue eyes. Fully jointed including neck,. MARKS: Japenese script "T" in triangle/12. $9.00

ITALY

6½" "LULU" shown in regional costume which is an extra outfit no. 3132. $4.00

6" "HANK" All vinyl. Black glued on hair. Painted teeth. MARKS: K, in diamond on head. MADE IN JAPAN, on feet. $2.00

8" "ALVIN" All vinyl. Glued white hair. Jointed neck only. MARKS: K, in diamond on head. MADE IN JAPAN, on foot. $2.00

VIETNAM

15" "SOUVENIR DOLL" Plastic with untinted head. Glued on yarn hair. Painted features. MARKS: none. 1971. $8.00

GENERAL MILLS
HASBRO
HOLIDAY FAIR
HOLLYWOOD DOLLS

15" LITTLE MISS NO NAME. Rigid vinyl with inset large round eyes. Tear drop on left cheek. MARKS: 1965 HASBRO. $45.00

12" G.I.JOE. These first ones came looking like (features) of different countries. MARKS: GI JOE/COPYRIGHT 1964/BY HASBRO/PAT. NO. 3277602/MADE IN U. S. A., on right hip. $22.00

12" G.I.JOE NURSE. Fully jointed (elbows, wrists, knees, ankles) vinyl. Rooted side parted short blonde hair. MARKS: HASBRO /MADE IN U.S.A. $22.00

9½" PETEENA. (Poodle dog). All jointed vinyl. Painted brown eyes with inset plastic lashes. Straight legs and poodle tail. MARKS: 1966/HASBRO/JAPAN/PATENT PENDING. $4.00

21" THAT KID. Rigid vinyl body & limbs. Vinyl head. Open/closed moutn, molded upper teeth. Freckles. Battery operated. MARKS: HASBRO/1967. $18.00

18" AIMEE. Plastic & vinyl with jointed waist. Brown sleep eyes. Smile closed mouth. Came with extra hair pieces. MARKS: HASBRO INC/1972. $20.00

9" CANDY BABIES: DOTS, PEPPERMINT PATTIE, BABY RUTH & CHOO CHOO CHARLIE. Stuffed bean bag bodys. Vinyl heads & gauntlet hands. Rooted hair. Painted eyes. 1972. $7.00

10" LEGGY (Kate, Nan, Sue & Jill). All jointed vinyl. Very long thin legs. Painted eyes. MARKS: 1972/HASBRO/HONG KONG. $6.00

5" FLYING NUN. All vinyl with rooted hair & painted features. White nun habit. MARKS: 1967/HASBRO/HONG KONG. $9.00

6½" WATER LILY. One piece molded body in sitting position. Hands crossed at chest. Painted features. Watermelon smile mouth. Blonde hair. MARKS: HOLIDAY FAIR INC./1967 JAPAN $4.00

6½" ELVIRA. One piece molded body with arms behind back. Painted features. Watermelon smile mouth. Freckles. Dark hair. MARKS: HOLIDAY FAIR INC./1968 JAPAN. $4.00

HOLLYWOOD DOLLS are well marked. Came in bisque, composition and hard plastic.

HOLLYWOOD DOLLS: BISQUE: $16.00

HOLLYWOOD DOLLS: COMPOSITION: $10.00

HOLLYWOOD DOLLS: HARD PLASTIC: $8.00

6" "SIPPIN' SAM & SUE" Plastic & vinyl with molded red hair. Green star eyes. Open mouth /not nurser. Dimples. Original. MARKS: 1972/GENERAL MILLS /FUN GROUP INC. $2.00 each.

14" "PEEK-A-BOO". Plastic body with vinyl arms, legs and head. Painted blue eyes. Original. Pull string operated. Puts blanket up to eyes. MARKS: HASBRO IND./ 1972. $20.00

HOLIDAY FAIR

6½" "LUVA BOY" Plastic body. Jointed neck only. Vinyl head. LEFT: Red-orange hair. Green navel. MARKS: MADE IN HONG KONG. 1966. RIGHT: Green hair, original. $2.00 each.

5" "QUEEN FOR A DAY" 1946. Jointed neck, shoulders and hips. White shoes. MARKS: MFG. CO./ TO MUTUAL BROADCASTING SYSTEM/QUEEN FOR A DAY/ STARRING JACK BAILEY.$22.00

16" BABY BUMPS. Compo. head with painted blue eyes. Open /closed mouth. Flange neck. Muslin body. Pink sateen arms & legs. MARKS: E.I.H.CO.INC. White $60.00. Black $75.00

18" SLEEP DOLLY. Cloth body. Compo. head and limbs. Open mouth/teeth & tongue. Reddish mohair wig. Blue tin sleep eyes/lashes. MARKS E I H A D C, backwards on head. $65.00

10½" HEEBEE OR SHEBEE. All composition with painted blue eyes. Molded on dress & booties. Jointed shoulders only. No hair or brows. $90.00

21" GOLD MEDAL BABY. Cloth body. Compo. head & limbs. Molded-painted hair. Green sleep eyes. Open/closed mouth /two upper & lower teeth. MARKS: E.I.H.Co. $50.00

19" ROSEBUD. Cloth body. Compo. Swivel shoulder head, arms & legs. Tin sleep eyes. Dimples. Open mouth/three teeth & tongue. MARKS: ROSEBUD. $37.50

22" BABY DIMPLES. Cloth body. Compo. arms, legs, swivel shoulder, head. Sleep eyes where eye opening cut so part of pupil is covered. Open mouth/two teeth. MARKS: E. I. H.Co. INC. on head. $45.00

20" LAUGHING DIMPLES. Cloth body. Compo. arms, legs and swivel shoulder head. Same eyes as Dimples. Open/closed laughing mouth/painted teeth. Molded painted, yellow hair. MARKS: E.I.H. CO. INC. $55.00

16" BUTTERCUP. Rubber body & limbs. All fingers seperate with outstreched arms. Compo. head. Sleep eyes. Molded hair. Open /closed mouth with bottom molded teeth. $35.00

14" JEANNE HORSMAN. Cloth body. Compo. head and limbs. Molded hair in peak on top of head. Brown tin sleep eyes. Closed rosebud mouth. MARKS: JEANNE HORSMAN. $40.00

13" BRIGHT STAR. All composition. Fully jointed. Sleep tin eyes /black eyeshadow. Small open mouth/teeth. Straight leg little girl. $40.00

18" BRIGHT STAR. All composition. Mohair wig/stapled to head. Sleep eyes/eyeshadow. Open mouth/teeth. Straight leg little girl. $50.00

15" NAUGHTY SUE. All composition. Brown side glance sleep eyes. Open/closed mouth. Molded-painted brown hair with tall top knot. MARKS: 1937 HORSMAN. $65.00

13" JO JO. All composition. Blue sleep eyes. Chubby toddler. Came with molded as well as molded hair. Open/closed mouth. MARKS: HORSMAN JOJO/1937. $35.00

Left: 23" Composition flange neck on cloth body. Composition full arms and legs. Sleep eyes. Right: 22" Composition head with hazel sleep eyes. Cloth body with gauntlet composition hands & legs. Open mouth/2 teeth. $30.00

18" "CUDDLY BABY" Cloth body that is tightly stuffed. Composition bent baby legs. Sleep blue tin eyes. Open mouth/seperate tongue. Original. 1935. MARKS: H. C., on head. $40.00

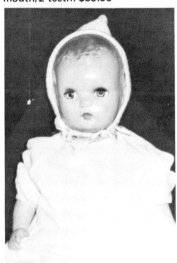

23" "BABY CHUBBY" also "RUTHY BABY" in 1940. Cloth and composition. Eye shadow. MARKS: A. HORSMAN, on head. $20.00

19" "BETTY ANN" Cloth body with hard plastic head, arms and legs. Open mouth. Eye shadow. MARKS: HORSMAN DOLL, on head. 1951. $12.00

17" CHUBBY BABY. All composition. Sleep eyes/lashes. Open mouth/teeth & tongue. Seperate fingers. Straight legs. Mohair wig in full bangs. MARKS: HORSMAN. $35.00

14" BI-BYE BABY. Early vinyl hands & head. Puckered face with open/closed mouth with molded tongue. Small painted eyes. Body is an open mitt for child to use as puppet. MARKS: HORSMAN, on head. $14.00

21" MAMA DOLL KEY WIND. Cloth body, soft early vinyl arms & legs. Composition head. Blue sleep eyes. Open mouth/two teeth & tongue. Mohair wig. Key-wind cries when put down, stops when picked up. MARKS: HORSMAN, on head. $35.00

20" TODDLER DIMPLES. Cloth body. Composition arms, legs & head. Molded-painted yellow hair. Blue sleep eyes. Open mouth /two teeth. Fat straighter legs than the baby. MARKS: DIMPLES, on head. $55.00

18" CINDY THE COUTURIER DOLL. Hard plastic body. Jointed waist & knees. Vinyl head. Sleep eyes. Rooted hair. High-heel feet. 1957. MARKS: HORSMAN/88, on head. $9.00

14" RUTHIE. Stuffed vinyl one piece body & limbs. Rooted red hair. Sleep eyes. Closed mouth. 1956. MARKS: 21 (backward) /HORSMAN/111, on head. $8.00

35" BETTY JANE. Rigid plastic body & limbs. Vinyl head. Rooted long hair. Painted eyes with inset lashes. Eyes glance to the side. MARKS: HORSMAN DOLL INC. $45.00

10" TEENSIE TINY BABY. Full jointed vinyl. Blue painted eyes. Open/closed mouth. Molded-painted hair. MARKS: HORSMAN DOLL MFG. CO./19/12. $3.00

16" MADEMOISELLE DOLLS. Rigid plastic body & legs. Vinyl arms & head. Sleep eyes. Closed mouth. Dolls were elaboratly dressed with various fancy hairdo's. MARKS: 19/HORSMAN DOLLS INC./67167, on head. HORSMAN DOLLS INC./PAT.PEND. on back. $22.00

19" BABY PRECIOUS. Cloth body. Vinyl head & limbs. Rooted hair. Sleep eyes. Open/closed mouth with molded tongue. Very large upper lip. MARKS: 1963 IRENE SZOR/HORSMAN DOLLS INC, on head. $35.00

24" SLEEPY BABY. Cloth body. Vinyl head and limbs. Rooted hair. Painted closed eyes. Closed mouth. MARKS: HORSMAN DOLLS INC./1963, on head $20.00

16" JO ANNE. All jointed vinyl. Rooted red hair. Blue sleep eyes. Closed mouth. MARKS: HORSMAN DOLLS INC./1963 G116. $10.00

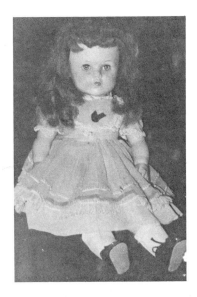

17" "SALVATION ARMY LASS".
All hard plastic. Blue sleep eyes
/lashes. Open mouth/4 teeth. All
original except shoes, includes
Salvation Army emblems and pin.
MARKS: HORSMAN, on head.
1953. $26.00

22" "ALICE IN WONDERLAND"
One piece early plastic body,
arms and legs. Early vinyl head
with rooted long hair. Blue sleep
eyes/lashes. Orininal. MARKS: 96
HORSMAN, on head. 1956. $22.00

12" "CINDY LOU" sold through
Winston Sales, Chicago & came
with 25 piece wardrobe and ad-
vertised in the "Workbasket" Dec.
1958. MARKS: 32/HORSMAN,
on head. $4.00

16" "CINDY" All stuffed vinyl
with rooted red hair. Blue sleep
eyes. MARKS: 82/HORSMAN.
1957. $8.00

12″  SWEET BABY. Plastic body. Vinyl arms, legs & head. Rooted hair. Sleep eyes. Open mouth nurser. MARKS: HORSMAN DOLLS INC/1964/B144, on head. $5.00. Also with pull string music and body mover (LULLABYE BABY) MARKS: B1441 /HORSMAN DOLLS INC/1967. $6.00

12″  SINGING PIPSQUEEKS. Cleo: eyes closed, oval mouth. Anthony: painted eyes to side, round mouth. Patty: blonde hair, eyes closed, wide open/closed mouth. Mark: Round painted eyes to side, mouth less open than others. MARKS: all have HORSMAN DOLLS INC./1967/6712 followed by two letters (FF, GG, etc) $6.00 each.

28″  ALICE IN WONDERLAND. Rigid vinyl body & limbs. Vinyl head with rooted long blonde hair. Blue sleep eyes. Closed mouth. MARKS: 1/HORSMAN DOLL INC/1966/66271. $45.00

11″  YES-NO TODDLER. (ANSWER DOLL). All hard plastic. Sleep eyes. Toddler legs. Has push button in stomach to make head move. MARKS: PAT. PEND. on body. $7.00

10″  ANSWER DOLL. Rigid vinyl body & limbs. Vinyl head. Rooted hair. Sleep eyes. Push button in stomach. MARKS: 66-100/7/ HORSMAN DOLLS INC/1966. $5.00

21″  SLEEPY. Cloth body, upper arms & legs. Early vinyl lower arms, legs, & head. Head stuffed. Closed eyes. Open, yawning mouth. Molded tuffs of hair. MARKS: HORSMAN, on head. $12.00

11   CHRISTOPHER ROBIN. All vinyl. Painted eyes. Closed mouth, rooted, side parted hair. MARKS: HORSMAN DOLL INC./ 66111. $24.00

25″  LADY DOLL. Rigid vinyl. Vinyl head & arms. Rooted dark hair. Sleep blue eyes. High heel feet. Very small waist. Adult hands. MARKS: HORSMAN/1961/JK 25/4. $30.00

20″  THIRSTEE. All vinyl. Round fat cheeks. Open mouth/nurser. Sleep eyes. MARKS: HORSMAN/1961/BCL8. $6.00

22″  MY RUTHIE. Plastic body & legs. Vinyl arms & head. Rooted blonde hair. Blue sleep eyes. MARKS: HORSMAN DOLLS INC./1964/216, on head. $5.00

14″  CRAWL BABY. Rigid vinyl. Vinyl head. Head adjusts by slot. Sleep eyes. Open/closed mouth. Hands flat, bent knees. MARKS: 2700/14EYE/3/HORSMAN DOLL INC/1967, on head. 25/ HORSMAN DOLLS INC./PAT. PEND., on back. $18.00

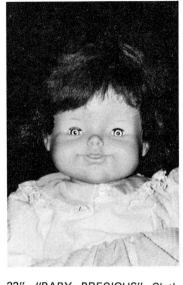

12" "TWEETIE" A Couturier Doll. Vinyl. Rooted hair. Sleep brown eyes/lashes. Had 2 pcs. Tweetie Toilettries tied to wrist. MARKS: P.J. on head. This doll is also "Peggy Ann". 1959. $8.00

22" "BABY PRECIOUS" Cloth with vinyl head and limbs. Open /closed mouth with heavy overlip. Sleep blue eyes. MARKS: 1963 IRENE SZOR/HORSMAN DOLLS INC. $20.00

20" "PRETTY RUTHIE" Plastic & vinyl. Socket head into body. MARKS: HORSMAN/T-21. 1963. Also Kindergarden Kathy. $5.00

16" "BETTY" Plastic body and legs. Vinyl arms and head. Rooted blonde hair. Blue sleep eyes/lashes. Closed mouth. MARKS: HORS-MAN/T-16 on head. 1965. $3.00

20" BABY TWEAKS. Stuffed cloth body. Vinyl arms, legs and head. Inset blue eyes. Rooted hair. Squeekers in arms & legs. MARKS: 54/HORSMAN DOLLS INC./1967/67191. $12.00

12½" BOOTSIE. Cloth body as well as plastic. Vinyl arms, legs and head. Sleep eyes. Rooted hair. MARKS: 2907/13EYE/T125/3/ HORSMAN DOLLS INC./1969. $16.00

16" BABY FIRST TOOTH. Cloth body. Vinyl limbs & head. Painted blue eyes. Crying mouth with molded tongue & one tooth. Molded tears on cheeks. MARKS: HORSMAN DOLLS INC./ 10141. $32.00

12" MARY & JERRY. Full jointed vinyl. Open mouth/nurser. Cries tears. Blue sleep eyes. Rooted hair. MARKS: HORSMAN/T1259. $7.00 each.

14" RE-ISSUE BYE-LO BABY. Cloth body. Vinyl limbs. Molded hair. Painted blue eyes. Open/close mouth. MARKS: 3, in square /HORSMAN DOLLS INC./1972, on head. $10.00

15" FAIR SKIN DOLL. All vinyl. Rooted long blonde hair. Sleep blue eyes. Closed mouth. Deep dimpled knees. MARKS: HORS-MAN/H-14, on head. S-16 on feet. 1960. $10.00

26" RUTHS SISTER. Plastic body & legs. Vinyl arms & head. Rooted hair. Sleep blue eyes. Posable head. MARKS: HORSMAN/T-27, on head. $25.00

16" BETTY JO. Plastic body & legs. Vinyl arms & head. Sleep blue eyes. Rooted red hair. Open/closed mouth. MARKS: HORS-MAN DOLLS INC./06183/4, on head. $16.00

17" POOR PITIFUL PEARL. Plastic body & legs. Vinyl arms & head. Sleep blue eyes. MARKS: 1963/WM STEIG/HORSMAN DOLLS INC., on head. $25.00

15" TYNIE TODDLER. Plastic body & legs. Vinyl arms & head. Rooted blonde hair. Sleep blue eyes. Open/closed mouth. MARKS: HORSMAN DOLLS INC./67165, on head. 1964. $3.00

14" BUTTERCUP. Plastic body. Vinyl limbs & head. Rooted hair. Sleep eyes. Open mouth/nurser. MARKS: 2316/13EYE/9/ HORSMAN DOLL INC/07151.1963. $3.00

16" TUFFIE. All vinyl. Rooted blonde hair. Blue sleep eyes. Upper lip over the lower one. MARKS: HORSMAN DOLL INC./B19, on head / body. 1966. $22.00

14" "MARY OF TWINS, JERRY & MARY" All vinyl. Rooted blonde hair. Sleep blue eyes. Nurser. MARKS: HORSMAN DOLLS INC./1965/B-90, on head. $2.00

11½" "RUTHIE BABY" Plastic body and legs. Vinyl arms and head. Rooted light brown hair. Dark blue sleep eyes/lashes. Closed mouth, protruding upper lip. MARKS: 34/07113/HORSMAN DOLLS INC./1967 on head. $3.00

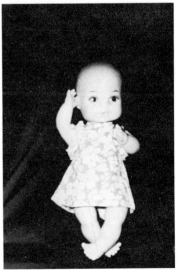

10" "BEAN BAG DOLL" Vinyl head and gauntlet hands. Freckles. MARKS: 3437/16/HORSMAN DOLLS INC., on head. TAG: HORSMAN DOLL INC. $2.00

9" "TEENSIE BABY" Plastic body. Vinyl arms, legs and head. Molded hair. Dimpled cheeks. Open mouth/nurser. MARKS: HORSMAN DOLLS INC/BC9 on back. $2.00

It is very rare to find an unmarked authentic Shirley Temple.

MARKS: COMPOSITION DOLLS: SHIRLEY TEMPLE, straight or arched. SHIRLEY TEMPLE/a number, or COP. IDEAL/N & Tco.

MARKS: VINYL DOLLS: IDEAL DOLL/ST and a series of numbers. All have the "ST". 36" is on the Patti Play-pal body.

COMPOSITION 25": All compo. toddler; MARKS: 73/SHIRLEY TEMPLE: $300.00. VINYL: 36" $280.00
COMPOSITION 23": Cloth body toddler: MARKS: Figure no. 1. $100.00 VINYL: 19" $50.00
COMPOSITION: 16" Baby: MARKS: SHIRLEY TEMPLE, on head: $125.00. VINYL: 17" $45.00
COMPOSITION: 17" Baby; MARKS: SHIRLEY TEMPLE, on head; $125.00. VINYL: 15" $35.00
COMPOSITION: 18" Baby: MARKS: SHIRLEY TEMPLE, on head: $140.00. VINYL: 12" $25.00
COMPOSITION: 22" Baby: MARKS: SHIRLEY TEMPLE, on head: $160.00. VINYL: 10" $25.00
COMPOSITION: 25" Baby: MARKS: SHIRLEY TEMPLE, on head: $185.00
27" Baby: MARKS: SHIRLEY TEMPLE, on head: $195.00
27" all compo: $200.00
25" all compo: $110.00
23" all compo: $95.00
22" all compo: $85.00
18" all compo: $85.00
17" all compo: $85.00
16" all compo: $85.00
15" all compo: $85.00
13" all compo: $75.00
11" all compo: $140.00
Any size Hawaiian: $110.00
"Soap" Shirley's: $30.00
"Plaster" Shirleys: $15.00
RELIABLE OF CANADA SHIRLEY TEMPLE: $45.00
Mechanical Display Shirleys: $1000.00
9" all compo. Molded hair. Closed mouth: IDEAL/DOLL on back: $60.00

11" "SHIRLEY TEMPLE" All composition. Original Texas Centenial Ranger outfit. $140.00

18" "SHIRLEY TEMPLE" All composition and all original. $85.00

12" "SHIRLEY TEMPLE" All vinyl 1957 issue. Original. $25.00

17" "SHIRLEY TEMPLE" All vinyl. Inset teeth. Flirty eyes. $45.00

19" SNOW WHITE. Composition shoulder, head, arms & legs. Cloth
body. Painted eyes to the side. Molded black hair with ribbon
molded in center. MARKS: IDEAL DOLL, on head. $45.00

21" DEANNA DURBIN. All compo. Dark glued on wig. Green sleep
eyes. Open mouth/teeth & tongue. MARKS: DEANNA DURBIN
/IDEAL TOY CO. $95.00 and up.

21" JUDY GARLAND. All compo. Glued on dark wig. Brown sleep
eyes. Open mouth/teeth. MARKS: IDEAL DOLL/MADE IN
U.S.A., on head. IDEAL DOLL/21 (backward), on body. $100.00

18" JUDY GARLAND. All compo. Large brown sleep eyes. Dark
wig in pigtails. Open mouth/teeth. MARKS: IDEAL DOLL,
on head. 18/IDEAL DOLL/MADE IN U.S.A., on back. 11/18
on upper left arm. 18, inside both legs. $150.00 and up.

17" HUSH A BYE BABY. Cloth body, limbs/rubber coating. Compo.
head with molded-painted deep yellow hair. Sleep eyes. Open
mouth. MARKS: IDEAL, in diamond/U.S.PATENTS/1621434/
162567. $65.00

22" BABY PEGGY. Cloth body. Compo. head & limbs (straight legs).
Flirty blue tin sleep eyes. Open/closed mouth/four painted teeth.
MARKS: IDEAL, in diamond. U.S. of A. $80.00

15" SLEEPY TIME TWINS. Cloth bodies. Compo. arms, legs and
heads. Painted features. One sleep/closed eyes & mouth, other
closed eyes and yawn mouth. MARKS: IDEAL DOLL, on heads.
$24.00 each.

16½" PETER PAN. Green felt suit is body and arms. Gauntlet compo.
hands. Compo. head with molded hair & tin sleep eyes. MARKS:
IDEAL in a diamond. $30.00

13" TICKLETTE. Cloth body. Rubber limbs. Compo. head with
molded-painted hair. Flirty eyes. Squeeze leg cryer. MARKS:
IDEAL, in diamond. $32.00

20" CURLY TICKLETOES. Cloth body. Compo. head (swivel),
flirty eyes, open mouth/teeth. Caracul wig. Rubber arms (seperate fingers) & legs (bent baby). MARKS: IDEAL in diamond.
$40.00

18" PRINCESS DOLL. Full jointed composition body. Mohair wig.
Flirty brown sleep eyes. Open mouth/three teeth. Dimple in chin.
MARKS: IDEAL/18. This is a S. Temple look-a-like: $45.00

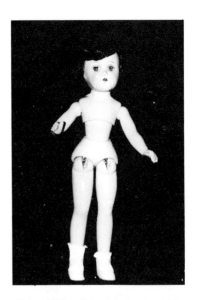

16" "NUN" All composition with brown tin sleep eyes. Open mouth /four teeth. MARKS: IDEAL TOY, on head and body. Ca. 1937. $30.00

13" "MISS WORLD'S FAIR-1939" Composition with wooden midriff. Green sleep eyes/lashes. Rosebud type mouth. MARKS: IDEAL DOLL, on head. IDEAL DOLL/ 13, on back. 10/13, back of left leg. $40.00

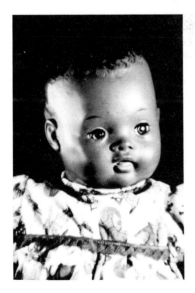

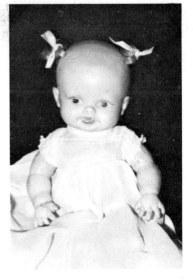

18" "SARA LEE" Brown cloth body. Early vinyl legs, arms and head. Sleep brown eyes/lashes. MARKS: Something that can not be read....17/IDEAL DOLL. 1950 $75.00

13" "BONNIE BRAIDS" This one has latex body with early vinyl head. Daughter of comic strip detective. MARKS: COPR. 1951 CHICAGO TRIBUNE/IDEAL DOLL/USA. $25.00

18" BETTY JANE. Full jointed compo. Tin sleep eyes. Open mouth /teeth. Mohair wigs Straight leg girl. MARKS: IDEAL DOLL/ MADE IN U.S.A. $30.00. Also 16" & 20". 1943.

16" BETTY JANE. Same doll as above but unmarked and in TAGGED VOGUE clothes. $45.00. 1943.

26" PRINCESS BEATRIX. Cloth body. Flirty sleep eyes. Compo. head & limbs. Molded-painted hair. 2nd & 3rd fingers curled on right hand. All curled on left. MARKS: IDEAL DOLL/MADE IN U.S.A.. $30.00. 1938.

17" SARA LEE. Cloth body. Early vinyl head & limbs. Sleep eyes. Open/closed mouth. Early colored doll with Negroid features. 1950. MARKS: IDEAL DOLL, on head. $65.00.

20" PLASSIE. Cloth body, laytex limbs. Hard plastic head. Molded brown hair. Sleep eyes. Closed mouth. MARKS: IDEAL DOLL /MADE IN USA/PAT. NO. 2252077. Same head as BROTHER COOS. $22.00. 1949.

16" PLASSIE. Cloth body. Latex limbs. Hard plastic head. Mohair wig. Sleep eyes Open mouth. MARKS: P-50/MADE IN USA, on head. $22.00. 1949.

10" SNOOKIE. One piece latex body & limbs. Stuffed vinyl head. Molded-painted hair. Painted blue side glance eyes. Holes in ears, cries when squeezed. MARKS: IDEAL DOLL. $8.00. 1951.

16" BABY RUTH. Cloth body(waterproof fabric). Vinyl head & limbs. Sleep eyes. Open/closed mouth. Rooted hair. MARKS: 16/IDEAL DOLL. $20.00. 1952.

14" MAGIC SKIN BABY. Latex body & limbs. Hard plastic head. Sleep eyes. Pierced nostrils. Came with molded hair or wig. MARKS: IDEAL DOLL/MADE IN USA. 1950. $18.00

21" BLESSED EVENT. Also KISS ME. 1950 & '51. Cotton body with plunger in back that makes her cry, pout or pucker. Vinyl head and limbs. Eyes are squinted almost closed. MARKS: IDEAL DOLL. $35.00

19" COLORED SAUCY WALKER. All hard plastic. Brown sleep eyes. Black wig. Open mouth/teeth. Straight legs. 1954. $65.00

16" SAUCY WALKER. Hard plastic walker body. Stuffed vinyl head. Rooted hair. Sleep eyes. Closed mouth. 1956. MARKS: IDEAL DOLL/VP17, on head. IDEAL DOLL/W16, on back. $25.00

14" "BABY RUTH" Stuffed oil cloth body. Stuffed vinyl arms, legs and head. Blue sleep eyes. Open/closed mouth with molded tongue. Cryer. DOLL MARKED: 95-14/IDEAL DOLL. 1952. $16.00

"THE MOST WONDERFUL STORY" All excellent quality vinyl. Jointed neck and shoulders. Inset brown eyes. Molded on swaddling cloth. Original. Doll not marked. Box: 1958/IDEAL TOY CORP. $45.00

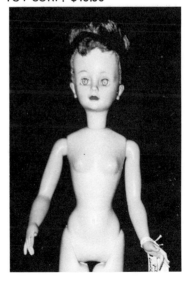

32" "SUPER WALKER" Plastic and vinyl. MARKS: IDEAL TOY CORP/BYE-32-35. 1959. $28.00

15" "LIZ" (LOVELY LIZ) also JACKIE-1961. Same body as used for CAROL BRENT. MARKS: IDEAL TOY CORP/G-15-L, on head. IDEAL TOY CORP/M-15, on body. $12.00

24" MAGIC LIPS. Vinyl coated cloth body. Vinyl arms, legs & head. Rooted hair. Sleep eyes. Open mouth/three lower teeth. Press back & mouth opens & closes. MARKS:IDEAL DOLL/T25. 1955. $40.00

25" MISS IDEAL. Plastic body & legs. Vinyl head & arms. Rooted hair. Sleep eyes. Closed smile mouth. Jointed waist, wrists & ankles. Also called TERRY TWIST. MARKS: IDEAL TOY CORP/SP-25-S. 1961. $45.00

36" PATTI (PATTY) PLAYPAL. Plastic body & legs. Vinyl head & arms. Rooted hair. Sleep eyes. MARKS: IDEAL DOLL/G-35. 1961. $55.00

18" TWINKLE EYES. Rigid vinyl body. Vinyl head. Rooted hair. Sleep eyes. Closed smile mouth with protruding upper lip. Dimples. MARKS: IDEAL DOLL/B-19-1. 1957. $12.00

28" SUPER WALKER. Plastic body & legs. Vinyl head & arms. Rooted hair. Sleep eyes. Closed mouth grin. MARKS: IDEAL TOY CORP./BYE S285. $45.00. 1959.

28" TRUDY WALKER. Same as above doll but MARKED: IDEAL TOY CORP./T28X-60. $45.00. 1959

38" PETER PLAYPAL. Plastic body & limbs. Vinyl head. Blue sleep eyes. Closed mouth/grin. 1960. MARKS: IDEAL TOY CORP. /BE-35-38. $85.00. 36" $75.00

28" SUSY PLAYPAL. Baby of the Playpal series. Plastic body & limbs. Vinyl head. Rooted hair. Sleep eyes. Open/closed mouth with molded tongue. 1960. MARKS: IDEAL DOLL/OB 28-5. $38.00

32" PENNY PLAYPAL. Also called Suzy Playpal. Same as above but MARKED: IDEAL DOLL/32-E.L. also marked: IDEAL DOLL/ B-32-B. $45.00

42" DADDY'S GIRL. Same doll as "Miss Ideal" but with straight wrists & small molded breasts. (figure of 12 yr. old) MARKS: IDEAL TOY CORP./G-42-1. 1961. $85.00

25" BYE BYE BABY. Plastic & vinyl. Molded-painted brown hair. Sleep blue eyes. Large open mouth/nurser. 1960. MARKS: IDEAL TOY CORP., on head. IDEAL TOY CORP./ HB 25, on back. $22.00

22" COLORED KISSY. Rigid vinyl body & limbs. Vinyl head. Sleep eyes. Rooted hair. Jointed wrists. Press arms together & she "kisses". MARKS: IDEAL CORP./K-21-L, on head. IDEAL TOY CORP/K-22/Pat. Pend. on back. 1962. $35.00

81

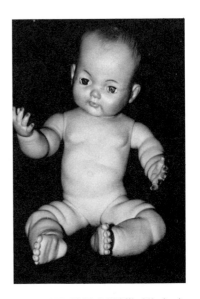

9" "OFFICER DIBBLE" Stuffed felt with vinyl head/molded on cap. MARKS: HANNA BARBERA PROD. INC., around neck. TAG: HANNA BARBERA/PRODUCT-IONS INC. 1962. $8.00

12" "BYE BYE BABY" All vinyl. Sleep blue eyes/molded lashes. Open mouth/nurser. Excellent modeling. Molded light brown hair. MARKS: IDEAL TOY CORP/12, on head & body. 1964. $4.00

16" "BABY GIGGLES" Plastic & vinyl. Raise arms and head tilts, eyes flirt and she gigles. MARKS: 1966/IDEAL TOY CORP/BG-18-H-118, head. 1968/IDEAL TOY CORP/BG-16, on hip. $25.00

9" "TEARIE DEARIE" All vinyl. Blue sleep eyes/molded lashes. Open mouth/nurser. MARKS: 1964 /IDEAL TOY CORP./BW-9-4., on head. IDEAL TOY CORP/1964 /BW-9, on back. $4.00

18"  GOODY TWO SHOES. Plastic & vinyl. Sleep eyes with long lashes. Rooted hair. Battery operated walker. MARKS: 1965 /IDEAL TOY CORP. TW 18-4-L-H4. This is the "closed mouth version". $25.00

27"  WALKING GOODY TWO SHOES. Same as above but with Open /closed mouth with painted teeth. Also a talker. MARKS: 1966 /IDEAL TOY CORP/WT-27-H-50. $35.00

15½" CAROL BRENT. Rigid vinyl body & limbs. Vinyl head. Rooted long hair, on top of head. Painted eyes to side. Molded eyelids. MARKS: IDEAL TOY CORP. /M-15-1, on head. IDEAL TOY CORP./M-15, on back. Made for Montgomery Wards. 1962. $20.00

18"  GIGGLES:COLORED. Plastic & vinyl. Rooted hair. Sleep eyes. Open/closed mouth. Press arms together & head tilts, eyes flirt & she giggles. MARKS: 1966/IDEAL TOY CORP./GG-18-H -77. $65.00

18"  COLORED GIGGLES BABY. Same as above with short hair and bent baby legs. MARKS: 1966/IDEAL TOY CORP./BG -18-H-77. $75.00

14"  BABY BETSY. Fully jointed vinyl. Rooted hair. Sleep eyes. Open mouth/nurser. MARKS: 1965/IDEAL TOY CORP./TD 14-W PAT. PEND. $16.00

14"  BABY REAL LIVE LUCY. All full jointed vinyl. Rooted hair. Sleep eyes. Open mouth/nurser. MARKS: 1967/IDEAL TOY CORP./FL-18-3532. $8.00

18"  LILLIE THE POSIE DOLL. Wire foam body. Rooted hair. Inset eyes. Closed smile mouth. MARKS: 1967/IDEAL TOY CORP. /F-16-E-H-34. $6.00

30"  BETTY BIG GIRL. Fully jointed vinyl walker body. Vinyl head. Green Sleep eyes. Open/closed grin mouth with painted teeth. MARKS: 1968/IDEAL TOY CORP./HD-31-H-127. $45.00

23"  BIBSY. Fully jointed vinyl. Rooted blonde hair. Sleep blue eyes. Open mouth with molded tongue. Feed & she drools. After drink she bubbles. MARKS: IDEAL TOY CORP./D-20-1. $16.00

11"  TEARIE BETSY. All vinyl. Rooted hair. Sleep blue eyes. Open mouth/nurser. MARKS: 1967/IDEAL TOY CORP/BW-12-H-86. $6.00

22"  LITTLE LOST BABY. Foam body. Encased plastic legs. Stuffed arms. Vinyl three sided head. Vinyl gauntlet hands. MARKS: TAG: LITTLE LOST BABY/1968 IDEAL TOY CORP. $25.00

12" "DR. EVIL" The sinister invader of earth...Arch enemy of Captain Action. All light blue rigid vinyl. Has vinyl face masks. MARKS: 1968, Ideal, in an oval, H119, on head. 1966/IDEAL TOY CORP., on back. $6.00

5" "FLATSY" An original outfit. MARKS: IDEAL, in an oval/1969 /PAT. PEND/HONG KONG, on back. $2.00

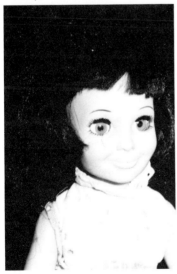

18" "TRESSY" Grow hair feature. Black hair & violet blue eyes. MARKS: 1969/IDEAL TOY CORP /GH 18/US PAT. 3162976, on hip. 1970/IDEAL TOY CORP/ SGH-17-HL6L/ HONG KONG, on head. $6.00

18" "DIANNA ROSS OF THE SUPREMES" Plastic and vinyl. MARK. 1969/IDEAL TOY CO., $65.00

16" MARY JO. Hard plastic body & limbs. Stuffed vinyl head. Glued on human hair. Sleep eyes. Closed mouth. 1952. MARKS: IMPERIAL, on head. $16.00

17" LINDA. Hard plastic body & limbs. Soft early vinyl head. Glued on Saran wig. Blue sleep eyes/lashes with painted lashes below eyes. Closed mouth. MARKS: IMPERIAL, on head. $20.00. 1951.

15" BABY PERRY. Latex body & limbs. Hard plastic head with caracul wig. Brown sleep eyes. Open mouth/teeth. MARKS: IMPERIAL CROWN/DOLL CO./MADE IN U.S.A., on head. 1955. $16.00

15" DOLLY, Latex body & limbs, Limbs attached with metal discs. Stuffed vinyl head with molded Dutch bob/full bangs. Inset blue eyes. Open/closed mouth. MARKS: IMPCO, on head. 1953. $4.00

13" SWISS FAMILY ROBINSON. ERNIE. Rigid vinyl body & legs. Vinyl arms & head. Rooted blonde boy hair. Blue sleep eyes. Closed mouth. Short pants with polka dotted shirt. MARKS: JOLLY TOYS INC./1962. $18.00

16" SWISS FAMILY ROBINSON. LOTTIE. Rigid vinyl body & legs. Vinyl arms & head. Rooted brown hair. Sleep blue eyes. Navy skirt/polka dotted blouse. MARKS: JOLLY TOYS INC./1962. $18.00

12" NOT ME. Rigid vinyl body & legs. Vinyl arms & head. Rooted carrot red hair. Painted eyes to the side with surprised look. Small oval closed mouth. Three painted lashes above eyes. MARKS: JOLLY TOY INC. 1963. $6.00

15" CHRISTY. Full jointed vinyl. Right arm bent. Large hands. Rooted hair. Sleep eyes/lashes. Small "OOH" mouth. MARKS: JOLLY TOYS INC./1965. $6.00

14" DIXIE PIXIE. Wire & foam body. Gauntlet vinyl hands. Vinyl head. Rooted hair. Sleep blue eyes. Open/closed mouth. Two molded teeth. 1967. MARKS: JOLLY TOYS INC. $5.00

15" COLORED SMALL STUFF. Same as white version on opposite page. Except has three tuffs of hair, and marked; 7/JOLLY TOYS INC./1960. $12.00

14" TIMMY. Wire & foam. Vinyl gauntlet hands. Vinyl head. Rooted hair. Painted blue eyes. Freckles. Pouty mouth. MARKS: JOLLY TOYS INC./1967. $5.00

20" LINDA. Plastic body, arms & legs, vinyl head. Rooted hair. Brown sleep eyes. Open mouth/nurser. Bent baby legs. MARKS: JOLLY TOYS INC/1969/16. White $7.00. Colored $9.00

**IMPERIAL CROWN**

18" "TINA" All vinyl with sleep blue eyes/lashes. Original dress. MARKS: 17-66, on head. 18-5 -B, on body. 1959. $8.00

**JOLLY TOYS**

13" "SHERRY LOU" Plastic with vinyl head. Sleep vivid blue eyes/ long lashes. MARKS: MADE IN HONG KONG, on back. JOLLY TOY, on head. $6.00

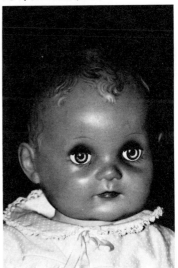

**JOLLY TOYS**

14½" "SMALL STUFF" Plastic and vinyl. Painted brown hair with one row of rooted hair. Blue sleep eyes. Also came in a black version. MARKS: 16/JOLLY TOYS, INC./1960. $12.00

**IMPERIAL CROWN**

25" "LITTLE MISS MARY LOU" All stuffed early vinyl. Metal disc jointed shoulders. Sleep blue eyes /hair lashes. Black eyeshadow. Molded light brown hair. MARKS: IMPCO, on head. Ads read: "MARY LOU LOVES U". $22.00

18″ CRUMPET. Plastic body & limbs. Jointed waist & wrists. Vinyl head. Rooted long blonde hair. Sleep eyes. Smile mouth.MARKS: 1970/KENNER PRODUCTS CO/235-225, on head. $7.00

12″ MAD CAP MOLLY. Flat vinyl head, legs & arms. Key wind walker. Molded hair, clothes & shoes. Painted very large eyes. MARKS: KENNER PRODUCTS CO./1970. $4.00

6½″ GARDEN GALS. Fully jointed vinyl. Bent right arm with partly closed hand to hold watering can. Painted features. Rooted hair. MARIGOLD: blond. BACHELOR BUTTON: brunette. ZINNIAS: lt. red. MARKS: GARDEN GAL/BY/KENNER/ HONG KONG. $4.00

9″ JENNY JONE & 2½″ BABY JOHN. JENNY: fully posable/ bendable vinyl. Rooted hair & painted features. JOHN: open/ nurser. MARKS: 1973 G.M.F.G. INC./KENNER PRODUCTS, DIV./CINTI. O 45202/MADE IN HONG KONG. $10.00 pair.

14″ BABY YAWNIE. COLORED VERSION. See illustration on opposite page for White version. $18.00

18″ NANCY NONSENSE. WHITE VERSION. See illustration on opposite page for Colored version. $12.00

13″ BETTY CROCKER. Stuffed litho. cloth. Very large eyes. Layered hair. Removable checkered dress and white apron. TAG: BETTY CROCKER/1973 GENERAL MILLS FUN GROUP/BY KENNER. $12.00

18″ GABBIGALE. COLORED VERSION. Plastic & vinyl. Painted eyes. Rooted hair. Pull string tape recorder talker. MARKS: GABBIGALE/1972 GENERAL MILLS/FUN GROUP INC/ BY KENNER. $10.00

16″ BABY CINDERELLA. Double face vinyl doll. One side with molded top knot hair. Other side with molded crown on head. TAG: KNICKERBOCKER TOYS. $6.00

12″ BABY AWAKE & BABY ASLEEP. Double face doll. Stuffed cloth with vinyl face masks. Painted features. MARKS: KNICK-ERBOCKER TOYS, on tag. $5.00

14″ BOZO THE CLOWN. Stuffed plush body. Vinyl head. Molded painted red hair. Painted black eyes. Wide open/closed smile mouth. MARKS: KNICKERBOCKER/TOY CO. INC. /NEW YORK USA, etc. OTHER SIDE: BOZO/THE/CLOWN/CAPITOL RECORDS/LARRY HARMON PICTURES CORP. 1963. $6.00

18" "NANCY NONSENSE"
Painted freckles across nose. Pull
string, located under left arm.
Speaker grill in chest. MARKS:
KENNER PRODUCTS CO/1974,
on head. $18.00

15" "BABY YAWNIE" All poly-
ester covered and filled. Vinyl
head with sleep blue eyes. TAG:
BABY YAWNIE/1974 G.M.F.G.I.
/KENNER PRODUCTS/MADE IN
TAIWAN. $12.00

12" "INDIAN" All plush body,
arms & legs. Vinyl head. Painted
features. Clothes top is removable. TAG: HUCKLEBERRY
HOUND TOY/KNICKERBOCKER.
1959. $4.00

11½" "TERRY TROLL" All stuffed cloth with non-removable
clothes. Vinyl head. String through
head for hanging. Metal discs in
hand and feet for weight. MARKS:
KNICKERBOCKER/1964/JAPAN,
on head. $10.00

20" CHATTY CATHY. See illustration for marks. Blonde with blue eyes. $10.00

20" CHATTY CATHY. See illustration for marks. Brunette with blue eyes. $12.00

20" CHATTY CATHY. See illustration for marks. Colored version. $75.00

25" CHARMIN CHATTY. Plastic & vinyl. Rooted hair. Side glancing sleep eyes. Takes records in side. MARKS: CHARMIN' CHATTY /1961 MATTEL INC. /HAWTHORNE CALIF. USA/U.S. PAT /PAT'D IN CANADA/OTHER U. S. AND FOREIGN/PAT-ENTS PENDING. $20.00

18" MATTY MATTEL. Cloth with hard plastic head. Painted features with side glance eyes. Pull string talker. MARKS: MATTEL, INC. /HAWTHORNE/CALIF. $18.00

18" SISTER BELLE. Cloth with hard plastic head. Painted features with side glance eyes. Pull string talker. MARKS: MATTEL INC. /HAWTHORNE/CALIF. $18.00

16" CASPER THE GHOST. Cloth with hard plastic head. Painted features with side glance eyes. Pull string talker. $18.00

15" TINY CHATTY BABY. Plastic & vinyl. Rooted hair. Sleep eyes. Pull string talker. MARKS: TINY CHATTY BABY/TINY CHATTY BROTHER/1962/MATTEL INC. /HAWTHORNE CALIF. USA, etc. Blonde $15.00. Brunette $22.00. Colored $75.00.

15" TINY CHATTY BROTHER. Same as above but with aqua cotton two button romper suit. Blonde $15.00. Brunette $22.00. Colored $75.00.

16" BABY PATABURP. Cloth body. Vinyl head & limbs. Sleep eyes. Open mouth. MARKS: TAG: QUALITY ORIGINALS BY/ MATTEL/BABY PATABURP TM/1963 MATTEL INC., etc. $9.00

15" SHRINKING VIOLET. Cloth with oversized head. Yarn hair. Pull string operates movable eyelids & mouth. MARKS: MATTEL SHRINKING VIOLET on tag. $45.00

18" BABY FIRST STEP. Plastic & vinyl. Rooted hair. Sleep eyes. Closed mouth. Molded on shoes. Battery operated walker. MAR-KS. 1964 MATTEL/INC./HAWTHORNE CALIF. MADE IN U. S. A. $10.00

16" BABY CHERYL. Cloth body with vinyl arms, legs & head. Root-ed hair. Sleep eyes. Pull string. MARKS: MATTEL INC/BABY CHERYL TM/1964. $16.00

BARBIE. In "BRIDES DREAM" No. 0947. 1962. Doll $10.00. Outfit $5.00.

20" "Brunette CHATTY CATHY" brown eyes. Pull string talker. MARKS: CHATTY CATHY 1960 /CHATTY BABY 1961/BY MATTEL INC. /US PAT. 3,017, 187/OTHER US AND FOREIGN PATS. PEND. $20.00

"MIDGE" No. 1012,1963 shown in her original box. For this set: $20.00. Doll alone: $7.00

21" "TALKING BOZO THE CAPITOL CLOWN" Foam body with pull string. Rooted orange hair (yarn). Painted features. MARKS: TAG: 1963/MATTEL/ BOZO THE CAPITOL CLOWN. Original clothes. $6.00

17"  SINGIN' CHATTY. Plastic & vinyl. Rooted hair in side part. Sleep eyes. Closed mouth. Freckles. Pull string. MARKS: SINGIN' CHATTY/1964 MATTEL INC./HAWTHORNE CALIF. USA. Blonde $14.00. Brunette $18.00.

21"  SCOOBA DOO. Cloth with vinyl head. Rooted long hair. Sleep eyes. Eyeshadow. Pull string. MARKS: MATTEL/SCOOBA DOO 1964. Blonde $35.00. Brunette $30.00.

17"  BABY TEENIE TALK. Cloth body. Vinyl limbs & head. Rooted side part hair. Decal eyes. Open mouth. Pull string operates mouth. TAG: MATTEL/BABY TEENIE TALK/1965. $10.00

18"  BABY SECRET. Wire/foam/cloth body. Vinyl gauntlet hands & head. Decal eyes. Rooted hair. MARKS: JAPAN 1965, on head. TAG: BABY SECRET/MATTEL INC. $10.00

13"  CHEERFUL TEARFUL. Plastic & vinyl. Rooted hair. Decal eyes. Open mouth that changes expression by left arm. MARKS: 1965/MATTEL INC./HAWTHORNE CALIF/US PATENTS PENDING/3036-014-1. $8.00

14½" TINY BABY PATABURP. Same construction, etc. as 16" listed. $9.00

17"  TEACHY KEEN. Cloth body & limbs. Vinyl head. Rooted hair. Decal eyes. Closed mouth. MARKS: MATTEL/TEACHY KEEN/ 1966/MATTEL INC. Sold from Sears only. $8.00

18"  BABYSTEP. Similar to Baby First Step (listed) but with short straight hair. MARKS: BABYSTEP/MATTEL INC./1966. Sold through Sears only. $12.00

6½"  TINY CHEERFUL TEARFUL. All vinyl. Rooted hair. Painted eyes. Nurser. Press to make face change expression. MARKS: 1966/MATTEL INC./HONG KONG. $6.00

17"  BABY'S HUNGRY. Plastic & vinyl. Soft vinyl head. Battery operated. Eyes roll, mouth chews, wets. MARKS: 1966 MATTEL on head. 1966 MATTEL INC/HAWTHORNE CALIF. on body. $8.00

17"  BABY SEE 'N SAY. Cloth body. Vinyl head & limbs (soft head) Pull string talker, eyes & mouth move. MARKS: 1966 MATTEL INC. USA/US PATENTS PENDING, on head. TAG: BABY SAY 'N SEE/1965/MATTEL INC. $12.00. Colored $22.00

18"  BABY WALK 'N SEE. Battery operated, walks, skates, eyes move. Body similar to Baby First Step. Head like Baby Say 'N See. Sold from Sears only. $12.00

16" "PATOOTIE" Cloth body, arms and legs. Gauntlet vinyl hands. Vinyl head with painted features. Pull string talker. MARKS: TAG: PATOOTIE/1965 MATTEL INC. $4.00

3" "PRETTY PRIDDLE" Brown hair & eyes. Blue dress & ribbon. White lace trim. Pink vanity & stool. MARKS: 1966 MATTEL INC. $8.00 set.

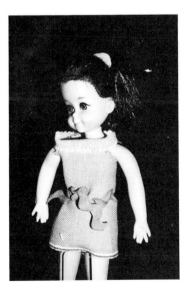

6" "CHRIS" friend of "TUTTI & TODD" Painted brown eyes. One piece body. 1966. $5.00

19" "CAPT. KANGEROO" Cloth. Pull string talker. MARKS: TAG IS GONE. MATTEL. 1967. $4.00

92

19" RANDI READER. Plastic & vinyl. Rooted hair. Open/closed mouth. Battery operated, eyes move back / forth. MARKS: 1967 MATTEL INC/US & FOR PATS PEND/USA. $20.00

18" TALKING BABY FIRST STEP. Plastic & vinyl. Rooted hair. Decal eyes. Open/closed mouth. Molded on shoes. MARKS: 1967 MATTEL INC, on head. 1964 MATTEL INC/HAWT-HORNE CALIF., on back. $12.00

9" BABY SMILE 'N FROWN. Same as Cheerful Tearful (1966) but has auburn straight hair, is 9" tall. $10.00

11" SMALL TALK. Plastic & vinyl. Rooted hair. Decal eyes. Open /closed mouth with molded teeth. Bent baby legs. Pull string. MARKS: 1967 MATTEL INC/JAPAN. $5.00

10" SISTER SMALL TALK. Plastic & vinyl. Rooted hair. Large Decal eyes. Open/closed mouth. MARKS: 1967 MATTEL INC. JAPAN. $5.00

15" DROWSY. Cloth with vinyl head & gauntlet hands. Rooted hair. Half closed decal eyes. Pull string. MARKS: DROWSY BY MAT-TEL INC 1966. $ THESE ARE STILL AVAILABLE. COLO-RED $8.00. STILL AVAILABLE. SPANISH SPEAKING $20.00

24" DANCERINA. Plastic with legs molded in "toe" position. Vinyl head & arms. Decal eyes. Rooted hair. Plastic crown on head. Battery operated. MARKS: 1968/MATTEL on head. $8.00. Colored $45.00

20" SWINGY. Plastic & vinyl. Walking doll that is battery operated. $12.00. Colored $60.00.

11" BOUNCY BABY. Plastic body. Vinyl limbs & head. Rooted hair, Decal eyes. Open/closed mouth. Spring action arms & legs. MARKS: 1968 MATTEL INC/MEXICO/US PATENT PENDING. $4.00. Colored $7.00.

10" BUFFIE. Plastic & vinyl. Rooted hair. Decal eyes. Freckles. Open/closed mouth with two painted teeth. MARKS: 1967 MATTEL INC/US & FOR/PATS. PEND/MEXICO. Holds 3½" Mrs. Beasley. Pull string. $12.00

16" BABY SING A SONG. Plastic & vinyl. Rooted hair. Decal eyes. Open/closed mouth. Pull string. Sold at Sears only. MARKS: 1969 MATTEL INC. MEXICO. $12.00

10" BABY GO BYE BYE. Plastic & vinyl. Rooted hair. Decal eyes. Open/closed mouth. Doll is strung. MARKS: 1968 MATTEL INC./HONG KONG. $5.00. Colored $12.00.

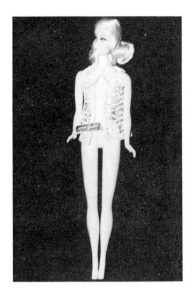

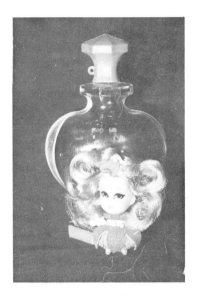

11½" "TALKING BARBIE" Pull string talker. Bendable legs. Lashes. Original. MARKS: 1967/MATTEL INC/US & FOREIGN/PAT. PEND/ MEXICO. $9.00

2" "KIDDLE KOLONE" came in LILY OF THE VALLEY, VIOLET, ROSEBUD, HONEYSUCKLE, SWEET PEA, APPLE BLOSSOM. $2.00

1967 MINI-KIDDLES POPUP FAIRYTALE CASTLE. $4.00

11½" "LIVE ACTION P. J." Brown eyes/long lashes. Bendable knees. Jointed waist and wrists. Bendable elbows. MARKS: 1968 MATTEL INC/US & FOREIGN PATENTED. $9.00

15" BABY TENDERLOVE. All one piece dublon foam. Rooted hair in skull cap. Painted eyes. Nurser. MARKS: 652X/1969 MATTEL INC. MEXICO. $3.00. Colored $6.00.

10½" VALERIE. Plastic & vinyl. Rooted hair. Decal eyes. Hair is floor length. Two painted teeth. MARKS: 1967 MATTEL/US & FOR. /PATS PEND./HONG KONG. $6.00

11" BABY WALK N PLAY. Rooted hair. Decal eyes. Two painted upper & lower teeth. Battery operated. Walks & arms moves to play with toys. MARKS: 1967 MATTEL INC./HONG KONG. $9.00

17" SING A SONG. Plastic & vinyl. Rooted hair. Decal eyes. Open/closed mouth. Pull string. MARKS: 1969 MATTEL INC. MEXICO. $10.00

16" TALKING BABY TENDERLOVE. All one piece dublon foam. Plastic ribbon on head holds pull string. MARKS: 677K/1969 MATTEL INC/MEXICO. $4.00. Colored $8.00.

14½" SHOPPIN SHERRY. Plastic & vinyl. Jointed waist, left wrist & thumb. Magnetic right hand. MARKS: 1970 MATTEL INC. /HONG KONG/US PATENT PENDING. $5.00

20" LIVING BABY TENDERLOVE. One piece foam head & body. Arms & legs attached with plastic holders. Nurser. MARKS: 140/1970 MATTEL INC./MEXICO. $4.00. Colored $8.00.

16" BABY LOVE LIGHT. Cloth with vinyl gauntlet hands & head. Battery operated, eyes light up when hand is held. MARKS: 1970 MATTEL INC. MEXICO. $6.00

12" TALKING TWIN. Cloth with vinyl head. Pull string. Two painted upper & lower teeth. MARKS: 1967 MATTEL INC/JAPAN. $4.00

20" CYNTHIA. Plastic & vinyl. Rooted hair. Decal eyes. Takes records. Battery operated. MARKS: 1971 MATTEL INC./HONG KONG. $8.00

16" BABY PLAY A LOT. Plastic & vinyl. Soft vinyl hands/jointed wrists. Pull ring & start switch. MARKS: 1971 MATTEL INC. /HONG KONG/US PATENT PENDING. $6.00

17" HI DOTTIE. Plastic body & right arm. Vinyl head & left arm. Plug in left hand. Decal brown eyes. MARKS: 1969 MATTEL INC. MEXICO. $4.00

11½" TINY BABY TENDERLOVE. One piece dublon foam. Glued on vinyl golden wig. Open/closed mouth. Decal eyes. MARKS: none. 1972. $6.00

11½" "TRULY SCRUMPTIOUS" in pale pink original dress. 1969. $12.00

13" "TALKING PATTER PIL-LOW" Stuffed. Pull string talker. MARKS:      MATTEL/TALKING PATTER PILLOW/1966. $4.00

5"    HIGH "DRUMMER" Cloth. Pull string talker. Arms hold drum stick. Says: "That's what I call a real crazy beat. Say would you like to join my band?" MARKS: MATTEL/TALKA-FUN/1969. $4.00

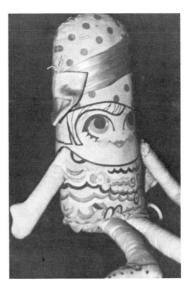

11" "ROARING 20'S" Printed cloth. Pull string talker. TAG: ROARING 20'S/1969 MATTEL INC., etc. $12.00

1959 BARBIE. Ponytail with curly bangs. White irses & pointed brows. Holes in feet with metal to stand on base. MARKS: BARBIE/ PATS. PEND/MCMLV111/BY/MATTEL/INC. $100.00 up.

1961 KEN. Flocked hair. Hard hollow torso. MARKS: KEN/PATS. PEND./MCMLX/BY/MATTEL/INC. $9.00

1963 MIDGE. Flip hair. Freckles. MARKS: MIDGE/1962/BARBIE (R)/1958/BY MATTEL INC. $7.00

1964 ALLEN. Reddish painted hair. Straight legs. $9.00

1965 SKOOTER. Twin ponytail hairdo. Freckles. $8.00. MARKS: 1963/MATTEL INC.

1965 RICKY. Reddish painted hair. Straight legs. $9.00. MARKS: 1/1963/MATTEL INC.

1966 TUTTI & TODD. One piece body & limbs. $4.00. Todd $8.00.

1967 TWIGGY. Very short blonde hair. Painted teeth. $9.00

6" DOCTOR DOOLITTLE. All vinyl with molded hair. MARKS: 1967/MATTEL INC./JAPAN. $8.00

22½" DOCTOR DOOLITTLE. Cloth with vinyl head. Pull string. MARKS: DR. DOOLITTLE/MCMLXV11 TWENTIETH CENT-URY FOX/FILM CORP. INC. $22.00

18" BEANY. Foam stuffed cloth. Vinyl head, hands & feet. Pull string. MARKS: MATTEL INC. TOYMAKERS/BOB CLAMPETT HONG KONG. $20.00

10" TATTERS. All cloth. Yellow yarn hair. Button eyes. TAG: TATTERS/1964 MATTEL INC. $15.00

21" CAPTAIN KANGAROO. All cloth. Pull string. Says 11 phrases. Sold through Sears. TAG: CAPTAIN KANGAROO/MATTEL INC. $10.00

11" THE MONKIES HAND PUPPET. Each finger is one of the Monk-ies (vinyl). Pull string. 1967. $6.00

25" DICK VAN DYKE. All cloth. Pull string talker. $22.00

16" SAUCY. Plastic & vinyl. Rotating left arm makes mouth & eyes change expression. MARKS: 1972. MATTEL INC. MEXICO. $9.00. Colored $18.00.

3½" "WET NOODLE" Came with various hair colors. Hair can be washed. MARKS: 1969 MATTEL INC/TAIWAN. $1.00

16" "TALKING TWOSOME" Cloth with vinyl head. Open/ closed mouth with two painted lower teeth. MARKS: 1969 MATTEL INC. MEXICO, on head. TAG: MATTEL/TALKING TWOSOME 1970 MATTEL INC. $9.00

11" "BABY BEANS" Vinyl head. Bean bag type. Vinyl gauntlet hands. One row rooted hair. Painted features. TAG: BABY BEANS /1970 MATTEL. 1970 MATTEL INC., on head. $3.00

12" "TRACY" Vinyl head. Decal eyes. Open/closed mouth. Two molded, painted upper & lower teeth. Pull string talker. MARKS: TAG: MATTEL/TALKING TWINS /1970 MATTEL. Other "twin" is TRISH. $4.00

16" TALKING MRS. BEASLEY. Lithograph all cloth. Yarn hair. Glasses. Removable dress. Pull string. $9.00

12" KING KONG. Cloth mitt with vinyl face. Glued on black hair. MARKS: KING KONG. TAG: QUALITY ORIGINALS BY/ MATTEL/KING KONG RKO GENERAL INC./1966 MATTEL INC. $6.00

14" MYRTLE of My Three Sons. Mitt with pull string. Vinyl head & hands. Decal eyes. Open/closed mouth. Yarn hair. Freckles. MARKS: 1969/MATTEL INC. $12.00

19" TINKER BELL. All lithograph cloth. Pull string. MARKS: MADE BY/MATTEL INC./HAWTHORNE CALIF. 1968. $4.00

12" WOODY WOODPECKER. Cloth mitt. Pull string. Vinyl head. MARKS: MATTEL/WOODY WOODPECKER/1962. $3.00

12" TOM & JERRY. Cloth mitt. Pull string. Vinyl head. MARKS: TOM & JERRY 1965/GOLDWYN MEYER INC. MATTEL. $4.00

12" POPEYE. Cloth mitt. Pull string. Vinyl head. MARKS: KING FEATURES/1967 MATTEL. $4.00

4" SKIDIDDLERS. (ANY) Snoopy, Donald Duck, Lucy, Goofy etc. $3.00 each.

11½"TRULY SCRUMPTIOUS. MARKS: 1967/MATTEL INC/US & FOREIGN/PATS. PEND/MEXICO. Pull string talker. $12.00

11½"TALKING P.J. MARKS: 1967/MATTEL INC./US & FOREIGN/ PATS. PEND./HONG KONG. Pull string talker. $9.00

11½"MISS BARBIE. Takes wigs. Has molded hair band. SLEEP EYES. MARKS: 1958 MATTEL INC./US PATENTED/US PAT. PEND., on hip. M. I., on head. $18.00

6½" ROCKFLOWERS. MARKS: HONG KONG/MATTEL INC. /1970. $4.00. Colored (Rosemary) $8.00.

11" ORIGINAL BABY BEANS. Bean bag body & limbs. Vinyl head with one row of rooted hair. Decal eyes. Pull string talker. MARKS: MATTEL/BABY BEANS/1970. $4.00

BABY DANCERINA. Same doll as the big one but not battery operated. $10.00. Colored $45.00.

17" CHATTY TELL (TIMEY TELL) Plastic & vinyl. Rooted hair. Decal eyes. Closed mouth. Watch built on arm. Pull string. MARKS: 69 MAT. INC. MEXICO. $14.00

"TALKING, BUSY KEN" Hands will hold accessories which were phone, TV, record player, soda set & travel case. 1971. There were two other "BUSY, TALKING" dolls, Barbie and Steffie. $12.00

4" "TEENER-LOREEN" No. 4003. Brunette in orange suit. MARKS: 1971/MATTEL/INC/HONG/KONG, on hip. $8.00 each.

11½" STEFFIE with brown eyes/lashes and hair. 1972. $6.00

11½" "MISS AMERICA" 1974. Came in blonde and brunette. Blonde $10.00. Brunette $8.00

11½" HADDIE MOD (also called MADDIE MOD). Plastic & vinyl. Rooted yellow hair. Brown painted eyes. Open/closed mouth. MARKS: MEGO MCMLXX1. $4.00

11" TANYA. Sun tan. Painted black eyes with lashes. Dimple. MARKS: MEGO CORP. MCMLXX/HONG KONG. $4.00

7½" ACTION JACKSON. Fully jointed action figure. Molded black hair. MARKS: MEGO CORP./REG. U S PAT. OFF./PAT. PENDING/HONG KONG/MCMLXX1. $4.00

12" BROADWAY JOE NAMATH. Solid vinyl full jointed action figure. Molded hair with long sideburns. Closed mouth. Painted eyes. MARKS: BROADWAY JOE/MEGO CORP. MCMLXX/ MADE IN HONG KONG. $12.00

24" MS FASHION. Plastic & vinyl. Jointed waist. Rooted white hair. Set blue eyes. MARKS: HONG KONG, head & lower & upper back. Large hips. 1973. $9.00

19" LAINIE. Plastic & vinyl. Jointed waist. Blonde hair. Painted blue eyes. Battery operated. MARKS: MEGO CORP. 1973/MADE IN HONG KONG, on head. MEGO, in circle/MEGO CORP 1973/ N.Y. N. Y. 10010/PAT. PEND. 327,304/MADE IN USA, on back. $15.00. Colored $35.00.

7½" DINAH-MITE. Plastic & vinyl. Fully jointed action figure. Rooted hair. Painted eyes. MARKS: MEGO CORP./MCMLXX11 /PAT. PENDING/MADE IN/HONG KONG, on back. MEGO CORP/1972, on head. $4.00

8" RIDDLER ARCH ENEMY. MARKS: NPP INC. 1973, on head. Still available.

8" SHAZAM. MARKS: MEGO/CORP/REG. US PAT. OFF/PAT. PENDING/HONG KONG/MCMLXX1. N.P.P. 1973. Still available.

8" CAPTAIN AMERICA. MARKS: MCG 1973 on head. Still available.

8" JOKER. NPP Inc. 1973, on head. Still available.

8" PENQUIN. MARKS: NNP 1973, on head. Still available.

7½" "DON" Dinah-Mites boy friend. Also used as one version of "Action Jackson". MARKS: MEGO CORP/REG. US PAT. OFF./PATS. PENDING/HONG KONG/MCML-XX1, on back. $4.00

8" "WILD BILL HICKOK" Fully jointed. Original. MARKS: MEGO CORP 1973, on head. MEGO CORP/REG. U. S. PAT. OFF./ PAT. PENDING/HONG KONG/ MCMLXX1. Still available.

8" "MR. MXYZPTLK" Arch-enemy for Batman. This is to show the two different faces that Mego used for this doll. Right $2.00. Left $9.00

8" "ACTION JACKSON" with mod hair & beard. Fully jointed Action Figure. Original, includes plastic dog-tag with his name. MARKS: MEGO CORP/REG. U.S. PAT OFF./PAT. PENDING/HONG KONG/MCMLXX1. $4.00

15" VERONICA. By monica Studios. All composition. Rooted human hair. Painted blue eyes. MARKS: none. $60.00

17" MONICA. (Monica Studios.) All composition. Rooted human dark brown hair. Painted blue eyes. MARKS: None. $65.00

20" ROSALIND. (Monica Studios.) All composition. Rooted light brown hair. Painted brown eyes. MARKS: none. $75.00

22" MONICA JOAN. (Monica Studios). All composition. Rooted blonde hair. Painted blue eyes. MARKS: None. $75.00

24" MONICA LYNN. (Monica Studios). All composition. Blonde rooted hair. Painted brown eyes. MARKS: none. $85.00

14" ROSEMARY. (Monica Studios). All hard plastic. Rooted brown hair. Painted brown eyes. MARKS: none. $65.00

17" ELIZABETH. (Monica Studios). All hard plastic. Rooted blonde hair. Sleep blue eyes. MARKS: none. $75.00

18" MARION. (Monica Studios). All hard plastic. Rooted light brown hair. Sleep blue eyes. MARKS: none $75.00

8" BRIDE MUFFIE. All hard plastic. Sleep eyes. MARKS: STORY-BOOK/DOLLS/CALIFORNIA. $12.00

8" GROOM MUFFIE. All hard plastic. Sleep eyes. MARKS: STORY-BOOK/DOLLS/CALIFORNIA. $15.00

5" CINDERELLA. MARKS: STORYBOOK/DOLLS/USA/TRADE-MARK/REG. Bisque $12.00. Hard plastic $10.00.

5" ALICE SWEET ALICE. MARKS: same. Bisque $12.00. Hard plastic $10.00.

5" RED RIDING HOOD. MARKS: same. Bisque $12.00. Hard plastic $10.00.

5" MISTRESS MARY. MARKS: same. Bisque $12.00. Hard plastic $10.00.

5" LITTLE MISS MUFFET. MARKS: same. Bisque $12.00. Hard plastic $10.00.

5" QUEEN OF HEARTS. MARKS: same. Bisque $12.00. Hard plastic $10.00.

MONICA

11" "MONICA JOAN" Embedded hair. All composition, decal eyes. This is the smallest of the Monicas. $50.00

NANCY ANN

10½" "MISS NANCY ANN" Shown in aqua blue tagged dress with white trim. $12.00

NANCY ANN

7½" "LORI ANN" Hard plastic with vinyl head. MARKS: NANCY ANN, on head. Original dress. $8.00

NANCY ANN

10½" "DEBBIE" Hard plastic body arms and legs. Vinyl head. Jointed knees. Sleep blue eyes. Walker, head turns. MARKS: NANCY ANN, on head. $10.00

12" TRACY. Plastic & vinyl. Rooted center part hair. Painted blue eyes to side. 2nd & 3rd finger on both hands curled. Closed mouth. MARKS: HONG KONG, on back. $3.00

13" LUCY. Plastic & vinyl. Rooted red hair. Painted green eyes. All fingers spread wide. Open/closed mouth. MARKS: PLAYMATE, with picture of world/a star. $4.00

11" THERSA. Plastic & vinyl. Rooted white hair. Painted blue eyes. MARKS: HONG KONG, on head. BY PLAYMATE in a circle imposed on a world with star. $3.00

15" MAY BELLE. Plastic and vinyl. Rooted yellow hair. Painted blue eyes. Bowed knees. Closed mouth/the tongue out corner. MARKS: PLAYMATE, on head. $6.00

11" CARLA. Plastic & vinyl. Rooted twin ponytails. Painted blue eyes. Right arm bent. Left straight. MARKS: PLAYMATE IN WORLD. $3.00

14" STACEY. Plastic & vinyl. Rooted single ponytail. Painted green eyes. Short stocky body & legs. MARKS: PLAYMATE in world. $5.00

15" ANNALEE. Plastic & vinyl. Side part rooted white hair. Painted blue eyes. Long thin legs. 12 yr. old body. MARKS: PLAYMATE, in world. $6.00

11" LOUISE. Plastic & vinyl. Rooted curly hair. Painted half-closed blue eyes. Bowed stocky legs. Dimples. MARKS: PLAYMATE, in world. $8.00

13" ROSE. Plastic & vinyl. Rooted red dutch bob hair. Painted brown eyes. 2nd & 3rd fingers on both hands curled. MARKS: PLAY-MATE, on head. $8.00

13" PAULA. Plastic & vinyl. Rooted red hair on top of head. Painted green eyes. MARKS: PLAYMATE in star & world. $3.00

9" ANY DWARFS. Composition head, hands & shoes, rest wood & wire. TAG: WALT DISNEY MARIONETTES/NAME/BY MAD-AME ALEXANDER N.Y./ALL RIGHTS RESERVED. $45.00 each.

32" DWARFS. (23" head cir.). Composition. Painted features. Regular puppet features. Made by Pelham of England. $285.00 each.

11" TONY. Composition & wood. Painted features. Shock of mohair wig. MARKS: TONY SARG/ALEXANDER, on body. TAG: MADAME ALEXANDER/NEW YORK. $35.00

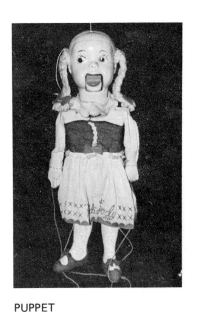

14½" "STACEY" 1972 - "COR-INE" - "STELLA" - 1974. Plastic with vinyl head, arms and legs. Right leg molded slightly bent. Sleep blue eyes/long lashes. MARKS: BY PLAYMATE, inside world in oval/7152, on back. **$4.00**

PUPPET

14" "HEIDI DOODY" Composition and cloth. $22.00

PUPPET

"WOLF GAL" Orange molded hair. Green painted eyes. MARKS: BOX: BABY BARRY TOY CO. $6.00

29" "MORTIMER SNERD" Cloth stuffed arms, legs and body. Gauntlet vinyl hands. Vinyl head with molded red hair. Painted blue eyes. MARKS: JURO NOVELTY CO. INC/1968, on head. Original clothes. $30.00

6"   BARRY GOLDWATER. Hard vinyl jointed at neck. Molded grey hair. Molded clothes, hat & glasses. MARKS: REMCO IND. INC. /1964. "Barry" button. $18.00

6½"   L. B. JOHNSON. Same construction as Goldwater. MARKS: 32/REMCO IND. INC. $18.00

9"   TRIPLETS. From My Three Sons. All jointed vinyl. Molded -painted blonde hair. Painted blue eyes. Nursers. MARKS: REM-CO IND. INC./1968/27, on head. REMCO IND. INC/1969, on backs. $6.00 each.

9"   PETTICOAT JUNCTION BABY (KATHY JO). Same doll as used for Triplets. $6.00

14"   BABY CHATTERBOX. Plastic & vinyl. Rooted white hair. Sleep black eyes. Open/closed mouth. Talker. MARKS: 52/REMCO IND. INC./E 116. $8.00

REMCO'S NEGRO LINE DESIGNED BY NEGRO ARTIST ANNUEL MCBURROUGHS:

     17"   TUMBLING TOMBOY: MARKS: 17EYE NEW/K26/REMCO IND. INC. $18.00

     14"   JUMPSY: MARKS: 3070/REMCO IND. INC./1970. $16.00

     15"   WINKIN WINNIE: MARKS: SE10/REMCO IND. INC. $22.00

     17"   BABY KNOW IT ALL: MARKS: 2955/17EYE/NEW/E6 /REMCO IND. INC./1969. $18.00

     17"   BUNNY BABY: MARKS: A. F. 3222BRS/E15/REMCO IND. INC. $16.00

     15"   BABY GROW A TOOTH: MARKS: REMCO IND. INC./1968. $14.00

     15"   BABY WHISTLE: MARKS: 1970 REMCO INDUSTRIES INC./HARRISON N.J. $14.00

     16"   TIPPY TUMBLES: MARKS: SM/E47/REMCO IND. INC. /1968. $15.00

     9"   TWINS: Same doll as used for My Three Sons Triplets. $12.00

     6½"   GROWING SALLY: MARKS: REMCO IND. INC./1966; $6.00

     16"   BABY LAUGH A LOT: MARKS: 3066/33/REMCO IND. INC./1970. $14.00

     15"   TINA: MARKS: REMCO IND. INC./1968. $20.00

     16"   BILLY: MARKS: REMCO IND. INC./1968. $20.00

     8" & 14" KEWPIES (1968 & 1969) MARKS: 7A JLK/2/CAMEO, on head. KEWPIE, on foot. 8" $10.00. 14" $16.00.

     12"   LI'L POLLY PUFF: MARKS: REMCO IND. INC./1969. $27.00

     8"   TINY TUMBLES: MARKS: REMCO IND. INC./1969. $14.00

13" "SNUGGLEBUN" Plastic body Vinyl limbs and head. Sleep green eyes. Cryer in back. Original clothes. MARKS: E 94/REMCO IND. INC/1965, on head. REMCO IND. INC./1966, on back. $8.00

16" "MUMBO-JUMBO" All blue plastic with vinyl head & felt ears. Removable clothes. MARKS: REMCO IND. INC./1968, on head. PAPER TAG:REMCO/MUMBO JUMBO. $3.00

19" "BLACK & WHITE MIMI". Battery operated singer with records. Refer to Series 11 of "Modern Collector's Dolls" for full description and clothes. White $22.00. Black $35.00

11½" "DUNE BUGGY BABY" Plastic and vinyl. Painted blue eyes. Button in back that makes her right arm "wave". MARKS: REMCO IND. INC./1972/HONG KONG. $4.00

18"   ROBERTA LYNN. All vinyl. Rooted black hair. Sleep brown eyes. Pierced ears. Flat feet. MARKS: 39-G-SB, on head $16.00

12"   CHARLEY. All vinyl. Molded hair brushed toward face. Large sleep blue eyes. Painted lashes below eyes. Closed mouth. MARKS: ROYAL DOLL CO/1964. $12.00

14"   MAGIC DOLLY. Vinyl head. Rooted hair. Sleep eyes. Nurser. Plastic body with extra joints at elbows & knees. MARKS: ROYAL DOLL/1961. $10.00

18"   SUE EMMA. Hard plastic (brown) body & limbs. Walker. Hard plastic head with black long wig. Brown sleep eyes. Painted lashes below eyes. Closed mouth. MARKS: ROYAL, on back. $18.00

22"   POLLY. (also 24"). Plastic & vinyl. Ball Jointed waist. Long neck. Blue sleep eyes. Open/closed mouth. MARKS: A ROYAL DOLL, on head. 1960/ROYAL DOLL. $12.00

24"   MARGARET'S DEBUT. Plastic & vinyl. Jointed waist. Rooted hair. Flirty green eyes. Open/closed mouth. Pierced ears. MARKS: A ROYAL DOLL/1960, head & body. $12.00

21"   LONELY LIZA. Cloth over foam body, upper arms & legs. Vinyl lower arms, legs & head. Rooted hair. Large painted brown eyes. MARKS: 1964/ROYAL DOLL. $25.00

11"   JOY. All vinyl. Rooted hair. Large painted brown eyes. Closed mouth. MARKS: A ROYAL DOLL/'65, on head. 1965/A ROYAL DOLL, on back. $8.00

23"   LISA TODDLER. Plastic & vinyl. Rooted hair. Sleep eyes. Open /closed mouth. Posable head. MARKS: 1962/ROYAL DOLL/ 3, on head. $6.00

19"   GRANNY. All vinyl. Rooted "salt & pepper" hair. Old womens modeled face. MARKS: 40-B-SG. Also: A ROYAL DOLL. $22.00

26"   BED DOLL. Cloth body, upper arms & legs. Plastic lower arms & legs. Vinyl head. Rooted hair. Painted eyes. Molded eyelids. MARKS: SAYCO DOLL CORP. $26.00

21"   POUTY. All stuffed vinyl. One piece body & legs. Molded hair. Sleep eyes. Very pouty mouth. MARKS: SAYCO/DOLL CORP. NYC/6U. $12.00. Rooted hair $15.00.

36"   DEBBY. Body & limbs of plastic. Vinyl head. Sleep eyes. Closed mouth. Rooted hair. MARKS: SAYCO, on head. 1961. $6.00

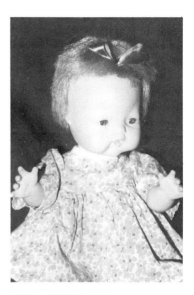

15" "ROBERTA WALKER" Plastic & vinyl with rooted blonde hair. Sleep blue eyes. Open/closed mouth. MARKS: AE 1504/15, on head. Original. 1966. $6.00

15½" "CUDDLESOM" Plastic & vinyl with rooted blonde hair. Blue sleep eyes. Freckles. Rosebud open mouth/not a nurser. MARKS: 1961 /ROYAL DOLL, on head. $3.00

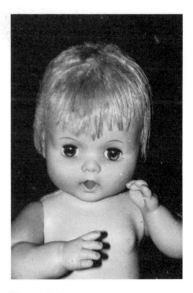

16" "LOVELY LINDA" All vinyl. Sleep blue eyes/lashes. Open mouth /nurser. MARKS: ROYAL DOLL /1960, on head. ROYAL, on body. $10.00

18" "CYNTHIA" Plastic body. Vinyl arms, legs and head. Large open mouth/nurser. Crys tears. Rooted hair over molded hair. MARKS: SAYCO DOLL CORP, on head. 1961/ALTER under left arm and back of both legs. $6.00

16"  TALKING TERRI LEE. All hard plastic. Painted features. Glued on wig. Phone jack attachment in base of neck (in back) to plug in record player. MARKS: TERRI LEE. $50.00

16"  TERRI LEE. All composition. Glued on wig. Painted features. MARKS: PAT. PENDING, on back. $45.00

16"  TERRI LEE. All hard plastic. Painted features. Glued on wig. MARKS: TERRI LEE, on back. $35.00. Colored $45.00. Brown $45.00. Orientals $50.00.

16"  JERRY LEE. All hard plastic. Painted features. Glued on caracul or wirey wig. MARKS: TERRI LEE. $50.00. Colored $60.00. Brown $60.00. Oriental $65.00.

16"  TERRI LEE. All very early vinyl. Weights in feet. Glued on wig. Painted features. MARKS: none. $35.00

10"  TINY TERRI LEE. All hard plastic. Glued on wig. Sleep eyes/ long lashes. MARKS: Circle C, on back. $25.00. Walker (head turns). $25.00

10"  TINY JERRY LEE. All hard plastic. Glued on lambs wool wigs. Sleep eyes/lashes. MARKS: Circle C, on back. $35.00. Walker (head turns). $35.00

12"  LINDA LEE. All early vinyl. Bent baby legs. Clothes with printed tags: LINDA LEE. Painted features. MARKS: Circle C, on head & back. 1951. $55.00

10"  LINDA BABY. All vinyl. Molded-painted hair. Painted black eyes. Open/closed mouth. Toes curled. Arms stick away from body. MARKS: none. $35.00

18"  CONNIE LYNN. All hard plastic. Slightly bent legs. Glued on caracul wig. Blue sleep eyes. Open/closed mouth. Toes are curled. MARKS: none. $45.00

9½"  SO SLEEPY. Loose stuffed body, arms & legs. Vinyl head. Molded-painted hair. Full closed painted eyes. MARKS: none. $30.00

16"  GENE AUTRY. All hard plastic. Hand brush painted hair. Decal blue eyes. Painted teeth. MARKS: TERRI LEE/PAT. PENDING, on back. $165.00

16" "TERRI LEE" All rigid plastic. Painted features. $35.00

" JERRI LEE" in dark rose satin cowboy shirt. White piping and pearl snaps. This is part of Jerri's Gene Autry rodeo outfit. Had striped western pants. No. 2858. $50.00

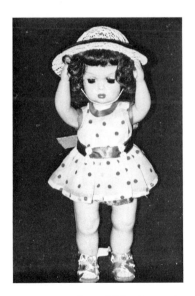

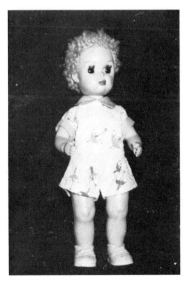

"TINY TERRI LEE" shown in her original red polka dot dress. $25.00

"TINY JERRI LEE" in "Pet Suit". The pet was a monkey called "Tony". $35.00

31" POLLYANA. Plastic & vinyl. Rooted white hair. Blue sleep eyes. Eyeliner. Painted teeth. MARKS: WALT DISNEY PROD./MFD BY UNEEDA/NF. 1960. $28.00

17" POLLYANA. All vinyl. Rooted white hair. Blue sleep eyes. Painted teeth. Molded-painted black shoes. MARKS: Same as 31". $20.00

21" PRETTY GIRL. One piece body & limbs of early vinyl. Vinyl head. Molded short bob hair/full bangs. Sleep eyes. Open/closed mouth. MARKS: UNEEDA. $9.00

18" BROTHER BOB. Latex body & limbs. Vinyl head. Molded very curly hair. Sleep eyes. Open/closed mouth. Molded tongue. MARKS: UNEEDA. $12.00

14" PURTY. All vinyl. Molded-painted hair. Inset eyes. Nurser. Squeeze chest & face changes. MARKS: 516-42/UNEEDA. (also 5/6-51 & 5/6-51( $16.00. Rooted hair $20.00.

23" COUNTRY GIRL. Hard plastic body & limbs. Walker. Vinyl head. Rooted hair. Flirty eyes. Open/closed mouth. MARKS: UNEEDA. $16.00. Colored $25.00.

11" DEBBIE. All vinyl Barbie type. Rooted hair. Painted black eyes. Molded eyelids. High heel feet. MARKS: U, on head. $6.00

15" SHIRLEY. Plastic & vinyl. Rooted dark hair. Sleep blue eyes. Painted lashes under eyes. Closed mouth smile. MARKS: UNEEDA DOLL CO/INC, in circle. /NC. $10.00

21" BABY DOLLIKINS. Rigid vinyl body & limbs. Jointed elbows, wrists & knees. Vinyl head. Molded hair. Sleep eyes. Nurser. MARKS: UNEEDA DOLL INC. $      With rooted hair $16.00

35" ROSY WALKER. Plastic and vinyl. Rooted hair. Sleep eyes. Closed mouth. MARKS: UNEEDA/37. 1961. $28.00. Colored $35.00

32" FAIRY PRINCESS. Plastic & vinyl. Sleep eyes. Rooted PINK hair with full bangs. MARKS: WALT DISNEY PROD./MFG. BY UNEEDA. 1961. $26.00

21" SARANADE. (also sold as Debteen Toddler - with different hairdo). Plastic & vinyl. Sleep eyes. Rooted hair. Talking mechanism in stomach. MARKS: UNEEDA DOLL CO. INC./1962. $18.00

14" BLABBY. All vinyl. Rooted hair. Sleep eyes. Open mouth. Press stomach & mouth opens & closes with cry noises. MARKS: UNEEDA DOLL CO. INC./1964. $18.00

13" "PETSY" All composition with painted blue eyes. Molded hair. One piece body and head. MARKS: none. 1940. $28.00

19" "SANDRA" One piece vinyl stuffed body, arms and legs. Vinyl head with rooted dark brown hair. Blue sleep eyes/lashes. Coo voice, will cry whenever touched. MARKS: UNEEDA, on head. Original. 1955. $12.00

32" "BABES IN TOYLAND". Same face as the Princess Doll called "Fairy Princess" from Walt Disney's Babes in Toyland. 1961. $22.00

32" "PENELOPE" Also same head as Pollyanna. Was sold with a large white poodle (plush) that was all white. 1962. MARKS: WALT DISNEY/MFG. BY UNEEDA. $20.00

8" WISH NIKS. All vinyl. Inset mohair wigs. Plastic eyes. Look like "Trolls". MARKS: UNEEDA/WESHNIK-TM/PATENT NO/D 190, 918. $1.00

18" WEEPSY WIGGLES. Cloth body. Vinyl arms, legs and head. Sleep eyes. Rooted hair. Key wind, plays music & doll wiggles. Also cries tears. MARKS: UNEEDA DOLL CO. INC./1963. $3.00

17" NANCY. Plastic body & limbs. Vinyl head. Rooted hair with full bangs. Sleep eyes. Closed almost pouty mouth. MARKS: UNEEDA/1964. $4.00

9" TUMMY-PUDGY PIXIE. All vinyl. Rooted hair. Painted eyes to side. Painted lashes over & under eyes. Fat tummy. MARKS: UNEEDA' $3.00

16" SURPRISE DOLL/BABY TRIX. All early vinyl. Pin and disc jointed. Mechanism in body makes head nod, feet kick & arms move. MARKS: UNEEDA. 1954. $22.00

12" PRI-THILLA. All vinyl. Rooted hair. Sleep eyes. Wide open mouth. Sucks thumb & blows up balloons. MARKS: 4, on head. $9.00

19" WIGGLES. Oil cloth outer body covering with vinyl arms & legs attached. Rooted hair. Inset blue eyes. Open mouth. MARKS: UNEEDA DOLL/NF 21. $55.00

32" FRECKLES. Plastic & vinyl. Same body as Pollyana. Large flirty sleep eyes. Freckles across nose & cheeks. MARKS: 22. $20.00

12" YUMMY. All vinyl. Rooted hair. Sleep eyes. Wide open mouth. Press stomach & mouth moves with sucking sound. MARKS: none. $16.00

10" CUDDLY BABY. One piece plush body. Vinyl hands & head. Rooted hair. Set blue eyes. Dimples in cheeks & chin. MARKS: 1961/UNEEDA DOLL. $1.00

23" MISS DEBTEEN. Plastic with vinyl head. Rooted hair. Blue sleep eyes. MARKS: U, on head. 1962. $6.00. Colored $10.00

20" BABY SWEETUMS. Cloth body with plastic arms & legs. Vinyl head. Molded hair. Sleep eyes. Open mouth. MARKS: 1962 /UNEEDA DOLL CO. $4.00

16" COQUETTE. Plastic & vinyl. Rooted hair. Sleep eyes. Dimple in chin. Straight toddler legs. MARKS: UNEEDA DOLL CO. INC. 1963. $8.00

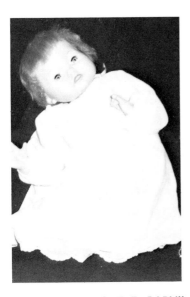

20" "MAGIC BOTTLE BABY" Cloth body. Vinyl arms, legs and head. Rooted ash blonde hair. Blue sleep eyes/lashes. Wide open /closed mouth. MARKS: 1962/ UNEEDA DOLL CO., in a circle. $6.00

11½" "PRE-TEEN BETSY MC-CALL" Red rooted hair. Sleep brown eyes/molded lashes. Plastic & vinyl. Shown in an original outfit. No marks on doll. BOX: 1963/UNEEDA. $15.00

16" "COQUETTE-THE SPECIAL GIRL" Black hair and blue sleep eyes. Original. MARKS: 4/UNE-EDA DOLL/CO INC./ 1963, on head. $8.00

16" "BABY TRIX" Foam with vinyl gauntlet hands. Vinyl head with rooted blonde hair. Sleep black eyes. Plastic neck flange. Original snow suit. MARKS: UN-EEDA DOLL CO INC., in a circle with 1964 beneath. $3.00

12"  BARE BOTTOM BABY. All vinyl. Molded hair. Sleep blue eyes. Open/closed mouth. Molded bent arms. Jointed waist. Lower body, legs in one piece. MARKS: UNEEDA DOLL CO. INC./ 1963. $6.00

11"  POSIN ELFY. One piece vinyl body & limbs. Vinyl head with crossed & slanted painted eyes. Molded hair. MARKS: UNEEDA DOLL CO. INC./1964. $2.00

11"  LITTLE COQUETTE. Plastic & vinyl. Slightly slanted blue sleep eyes. Rooted hair. Closed mouth MARKS: UNEEDA DOLL CO. 1964. $3.00

10"  POSABLE BABY TRIX. Foam body & limbs. Vinyl gauntlet hands & head. Rooted hair. Sleep black eyes. MARKS: UNEEDA DOLL CO. INC./3, in a circle. 1964. $3.00

11"  TINY TODDLES. Plastic & vinyl. Rooted hair. Painted side glancing eyes. MARKS: UNEEDA DOLL CO. INC., in a circle/1966. $4.00

11½"SECRET SUE. Plastic & vinyl. Rooted orange hair. Painted side glancing black eyes. MARKS: UNEEDA DOLL CO. INC./1966. $8.00

25"  ANNIVERSARY DOLL. Plastic & vinyl. Rooted reddish brown hair. Amber brown sleep eyes. Closed mouth. MARKS: 8/UN-EEDA DOLL CO/1967. $35.00

13"  FIRST BORN BABY. Cloth body. Plastic limbs. Vinyl head. Molded hair. Sleep eyes. Closed mouth. MARKS: UNEEDA DOLL CO. INC./1968/1468. $1.00

11"  DOLLIKINS. Rigid vinyl body & limbs. Jointed elbows, wrists, waist, knees & ankles. Vinyl head. Rooted hair. Painted eyes. MARKS: UNEEDA DOLL CO/MCMLXIX/MADE IN HONG KONG, on head. DOLLIKIN/US PAT. 3010253/OTHER US and FOR. PAT. PEND. $3.00

16"  BATHTUB BABY. Plastic & vinyl. Rooted hair. Sleep eyes. Bent baby legs. Nurser. MARKS: 3TD11/UNEEDA. 1969. $2.00

13"  ADORABLE CINDY. Plastic & vinyl. rooted hair. Sleep eyes. Nurser. Bent baby legs. MARKS: UNEEDA DOLL INC./MCM LXIX/MADE IN HONG KONG. $2.00

6½"  NEW BORN YUMMY. Cloth covered foam body. Vinyl limbs & head. Rooted hair. Painted eyes. Open/closed mouth. MARKS: UD CO. INC./HONG KONG. 1970. $1.00

117

15" "LINDA" Plastic with vinyl head. Blue sleep eyes. Lavender eyeshadow. White rooted hair. MARKS: D/30. Some are marked: U.D./30. $7.00

19" "MARI-GOLD" Black sleep eyes to the side. Blue eye shadow. Plastic and vinyl. MARKS: 8/ UNEEDA DOLL CO./1967/198. $7.00

8½" "PLUM PEE'S". All vinyl with squeeker in bottom. Unjointed with molded hair and painted features. MARKS: UNEEDA DOLL CO INC/1967/PLUMB*PEE 'S T. M. $2.00

14" "BABY BUNDLES" Dark pink vinyl. Cloth body. Sleep blue eyes. Rooted red hair. MARKS: UNEEDA DOLL CORP/1968/066970, on head. $2.00

118

12" MARY JANE. All composition. Blonde mohair wigs. Open mouth /two teeth. Sleep eyes. Made by Ideal for Vogue in tagged Vogue dress only. $32.00. MARKS: 13.

15" BETTY JANE. All composition. Blonde mohair. Open mouth/ four teeth. Sleep eyes. MARKS: 16, on back. Made by Ideal for Vogue. TAGGED DRESS ONLY. $34.00

10" JEFF. Plastic & vinyl. Molded brown hair. Sleep eyes. Closed mouth. MARKS: VOGUE, on head. $15.00

10" JAN. Plastic & vinyl. Rooted hair. Sleep blue eyes. High heel feet. MARKS: VOGUE, on head. VOGUE DOLL, on back. $7.00

10" JILL. All hard plastic. Glued on wig. Sleep eyes. Pierced ears. Jointed knees. High heel feet. MARKS: VOGUE, on head. JILL /VOGUE/MADE IN USA 1957, on body. $10.00

7" GINNY BABY. All hard plastic. Glued on lambs wool wig. Sleep eyes. Bent baby legs. MARKS: VOGUE, on head. VOGUE DOLL, on back. $18.00

17" BABY DEAR. Cloth body. Vinyl head & limbs. Rooted hair. Painted eyes. MARKS: TAG: VOGUE DOLLS INC. Back of leg: E. WILKINS/1960. $22.00. MOLDED HAIR: $26.00

25" BABY DEAR "ONE". Cloth body. Fat vinyl arms, legs & head. Rooted hair. Sleep eyes. Open/closed mouth with two lower teeth. MARKS: VOGUE DOLL/E. WILKIN. $30.00

25" BOBBY DEAR "ONE". Same as above but is a twin boy. $40.00

27" BABY DEAR "TWO". All vinyl. Very fat. MARKS: VOGUE DOLL/E. WILKIN. $40.00

8" GINNY & GINNY TYPE. All composition. $16.00

8" GINNY. Early non-walker $14.00. Early walker $12.00. Molded lashes/walker $10.00. Bending knee walker $8.00.

13" COLORED LITTEST ANGEL. All vinyl. Bent baby legs. Rooted hair. Sleep eyes. MARKS: VOGUE DOLL/1963, on head & body. $6.00

17" NEW BABY DEAR. Cloth body. Vinyl head and limbs. Rooted hair. SLEEP EYES. Dimple in cheeks & chin. MARKS: VOGUE DOLL/1964. 1960/E. Wilkin, back of leg. $20.00

20" "PONYTAIL TEEN". Plastic body and legs. Vinyl arms and head. Rooted orange hair. Green sleep eyes/lashes. Open hands with all fingers slightly curled. Not jointed at waist like "Brikette". 1960. $27.00

16" "BRICKETTE BY R & B" (Arranbee Doll Co.) Green eyes. Dark brown hair. All original. MARKS: VOGUE INC/1960. $32.00

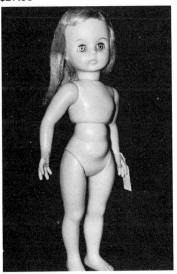

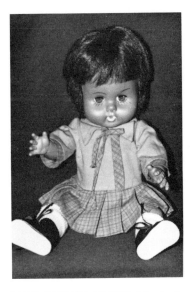

15½" "GINNY" Plastic with vinyl arms and head. Sleep blue eyes. Jointed waist. MARKS: none. 1962. $25.00

11½" "GINNY BABY" All vinyl. Brown sleep eyes/lashes. Open mouth/nurser. Rooted black hair over molded hair. MARKS: GINNY BABY/VOGUE DOLLS INC. $6.00